Lex Naturalis

A Journal of Natural Law   Volume 1   Spring 2015

Copyright © 2015
Pace University Press
1 Pace Plaza
New York, NY 10038

ISBN 10 - 1935625209
ISBN 13 - 978-1-935625-20-9
ISSN

Contributors
Address all submissions and correspondence to The Editor, LEX NATURALIS, Pace University, Department of Philosophy & Religious Studies, 1 Pace Plaza, New York, NY 10038. Please send two copies of the paper submitted. Include adequate margins, double space everything (text, notes, works cited, quotations). Use U.S. spelling and punctuation style (e.g. periods inside quotation marks; "double quotes" for opening and closing quotations). The University of Chicago Manual of Style, 16th Edition, is to be consulted regarding matters of style. Notes are to be numbered consecutively (in Arabic numerals) and placed at the bottom of the page.

Subscribers
LEX NATURALIS is published annually by Pace University Press, 41 Park Row, Room 1510, New York, NY 10038. Subscription price: $40. Please send all subscription inquiries to: PaceUP@pace.edu

Indexing and Abstracting
LEX NATURALIS is indexed in Philosopher's Index.
Copyright © 2015 by Pace University Press. Permission is required to reprint an article or part of an article.

Walter Raubicheck
Editor

Editorial Board

Harold Brown
Department of Philosophy & Religious Studies, Pace University

Michael Baur
Department of Philosophy, Fordham University

Gregory J. Kerr
Department of Philosophy & Theology, DeSales University

Robert Chapman
Department of Philosophy and Environmental Studies, Pace University

Alice Ramos
Department of Philosophy, St. John's University

Peter Widulski
School of Law, Pace University

Lex Naturalis

CONTENTS

VOLUME 1   **SPRING 2015**

Note From the Editor	Walter Raubicheck	
FEATURED ARTICLES		
The Effects of Accepting *Lex Iniusta non est Lex*: A Reply to Hart	Peter Furlong	1
The Natural Law, the Virtues, and Consequences in the Ethical Theory of Saint Thomas Aquinas	David Klassen	23
The Natural Law: Theoretical Insights and Prospects for Renewal from G.E.M. Anscombe	Zachary Mabee	51
Ars Legis: Reflections on Aquinas' "Christian" Articulation of the Natural and Human Law	Jeffrey Walkey	75
A Natural Law Critique of Mill's Argument for Justice	James Jacobs	93

Spaemann's Critique of Nuclear Energy: A Renewed Natural Law for the 20th-21st Centuries	Gregory Canning	117
Natural Law from a Catholic-Muslim Perspective: a Comparative Study of Jacques Maritain's and Abdullahi Ahmed An-Na'im's Philosophy of Law	Paola Bernardini	141

BOOK REVIEWS

Review of *Plato's Revenge: Politics in the Age of Ecology* by William Ophuls (The MIT Press, 2013)	Robert Chapman	157
Review of *Economic Justice and Natural Law* by Gary Chartier (Cambridge University Press, 2009)	Richard Connerney	163
CONTRIBUTORS		167
CALL FOR PAPERS		171

NOTE FROM THE EDITOR

Theories of natural law have been under attack since the Enlightenment, but still they recur in old and new forms within both the academy and in courts of law. The idea that human nature possesses an inherent sense of moral obligation no matter the culture, environment, or historical epoch is one that simply will not be eradicated by modern and postmodern assumptions about the varieties of nurturing and the physical basis of the mind.

Lex Naturalis intends to serve as a site for the ongoing philosophical and legal discussion of the courses of thinking and action that are called for when one applies natural law theory, whether it be Platonic, Aristotelian, Ciceronian, Thomistic, or Kantian in its orientation, or is a product of more recent twentieth and twenty-first century contributions to the tradition. The articles printed here testify to the vitality and variety of thought current within that community of intellectuals who cannot and will not separate ethics from the conclusions that have been and still are being drawn from the natural law.

Future issues will focus on particular ethical questions that challenge our contemporary world as well as on the relationship between natural law and related fields such as constitutional law and international law. A call for papers for our second issue can be found at the back of this first one.

THE EFFECTS OF ACCEPTING *LEX INIUSTA NON EST LEX*: A REPLY TO HART

Peter Furlong

In his influential work *The Concept of Law*, H. L. A. Hart, the great British legal philosopher and noted champion of legal positivism, levels several criticisms at the traditional natural law principle of *lex iniusta non est lex*. Although some of his criticisms have received a great deal of careful evaluation, others have not. In this paper I will focus on several ways in which Hart attempts to undermine the value of this principle, paying particularly close attention to his claims concerning the unfortunate effects that follow from either scholars' or ordinary citizens' acceptance of this principle. My goal is not to clear all possible objections to this principle, nor to prove conclusively its value, but merely to show that one set of arguments against it fails. Although this aim is surely modest, it is, I contend, nonetheless important. Investigating the relationship between morality and legality is undoubtedly one of the central tasks of legal philosophy. Since the time of Plato, natural law theories, although differing on various particulars, have proposed a powerful answer concerning this relationship. It is clear that these theories no longer receive the attention they once did, at least in part because of Hart's objections. I intend to show that these objections fail to show the inadequacy of the *lex iniusta* principle.

LEX INIUSTA: AN INTRODUCTION

Although there is clear precedent for the principle of *lex iniusta* in Plato and Cicero, the two most important thinkers for this present work who addressed this concept are Augustine and Aquinas. After discussing its history, I will move on to discuss two possible interpretations of the principle as formulated by Hart. I will then briefly consider the objection that the very formulation of this principle violates the common use of language. Finally, I will seek to locate the main criticisms that Hart levels against *lex iniusta* within the context of his overall criticism of the natural law project.

Before delving into the relevant sources of the formulation of *lex iniusta* criticized by Hart, it is worth dwelling momentarily on the earlier history of this principle. The general sentiment, if not the exact formulation, behind the principle of *lex iniusta* can be traced back to Plato and Cicero. In the *Laws*, the Athenian states, "We maintain that laws which are not established for the good of the whole state are bogus laws."[1] Cicero puts this principle into even stronger language. He writes, "Any other law [than that which is just] should not only not be accepted, but should not even be given the name of law."[2]

The formulation of this principle cited by Hart is attributed to the "Thomist tradition."[3] Although something similar to the formulation quoted by Hart is found in Aquinas's works, it is only found therein as a quotation of Augustine. Thus, before turning to Aquinas, it is worth mentioning Augustine's use of this principle. In *On Free Choice of the Will*, Augustine states (through the character of Augustine in the dialogue), "For it seems to me that an unjust law is no law at all."[4] Although there is debate concerning the force with which one should take this statement, the phrase "it seems to me" certainly seems to qualify the statement to some extent.[5]

It is now possible to turn to Aquinas's formulation of the principle, upon which Hart seems to be basing his critique. In his treatment of human positive law within the *Summa Theologiae*, Aquinas states that unjust laws "are acts of violence rather than laws; because, as Augustine says, 'a law that is not just, seems to be no law at all.'"[6] It is worth noting several things about this text. First, although it is a quotation from an authority, since it is quoted approvingly in the response, one can be confident that it mirrors Aquinas's own thought. Secondly, Aquinas adjusts or misquotes Augustine's words. In place of "it seems to me" he simply writes "it seems." If anything, this change might make this formulation of *lex iniusta* stronger than that of Augustine. Finally, although Aquinas's formulation is different from Augustine's, it is also different from the formulation offered by Hart as an element of the Thomistic tradition of natural law theory. Hart completely drops the phrase "it seems" and writes, "*Lex iniusta non est lex.*"[7] Such a formulation is found nowhere in Aquinas or Augustine, and there is debate concerning whether or not either author would endorse such a statement.[8] Whether Aquinas would formulate this principle in just these words or not is not a primary concern of this paper. Instead, I intend to investigate whether different interpretations of the formulation Hart offers can withstand his criticism. To this end, it is necessary to investigate different possible interpretations of the principle *lex inusta non est lex*.

The first interpretation of Hart's formulation[9] is conceptually the strongest and the hardest to defend. On this view, an unjust law is law in no sense whatsoever. It seems that it is this interpretation which best comes under fire when Hart complains that "the assertion that 'an unjust law is not a law' has the same ring of exaggeration and paradox, if not falsity, as 'statutes are not laws' or 'constitutional law is not law.'"[10] Moreover, it seems that such a claim would be incoherent.[11] Logically, it makes no sense to claim that all laws which possess a certain property (injustice) fail to be laws. The air of paradox can be dispelled if one realizes that this formulation is no more paradoxical than the claim that an invalid law is no law at all, a claim that is far less controversial than that of the natural law theory. Furthermore, one can then see that the logical formulation takes the phrase too rigidly. One is still left wondering, however, if this claim violates the common use of language. We will return to this question at the conclusion of section 1.

The second interpretation takes a slightly weaker stance concerning just how much is asserted by the principle, but it is also easier to defend against certain objections. On this view, there is some sense in which we can appropriately describe unjust laws as laws, however much they lack the fullness, perfection, or primary analogical significance of just positive laws.[12] This interpretation itself has several different varieties, ranging from complex interpretations relying on the epistemology and semantics of Aquinas' theory of analogy, to simple interpretations merely maintaining that some fitting characteristic of human positive law is missing in the case of unjust laws. Thus, one could gloss *lex iniusta* as "an unjust law is missing a property which all positive human laws ought to have." If one takes the latter approach, than it is possible to explain that the *lex iniusta* principle applies only to the central cases of law. John Gardner explains that restricting the central cases of law in this way does not mean that unjust laws exist in some gray area between non-law and law.[13] Instead, one must see that the shortcomings of unjust laws are failures precisely as laws. An unjust or immoral law is, according to Gardner, "a deviant case, and its study is logically parasitic on the study of its paradigmatic (morally successful) counterpart."[14] Thus, according to this interpretation, asking whether a law is just or not is central to evaluating it *as a law*.[15]

Having laid out these two interpretations, it is worth asking whether either of these views does violence to the ordinary use of language. According to the strong reading of *lex iniusta*, it seems that one should not call unjust commands laws any more than one should call counterfeit bills currency. One may call both of them false or imitation versions of the true thing, but that is as far as one's application of the terms "law" and "currency" should go.[16] On the second view, one can go quite a bit further. Although there is a central or complete description of "law" that some statutes do not fulfill, one may still call them laws in some attenuated or analogical sense. This second interpretation can therefore account for the actual use of the word "law" in describing generically all statutes (among other things) as laws, without regard for their conformity to moral principles. In any case, Hart contends that the issue surrounding this principle is "ill presented as a verbal one."[17] This charge against the principle of *lex iniusta* does not seem to be the one with which Hart is most concerned, and it is not one of the criticisms with which I am most concerned in this paper.[18]

Before turning to the main parts of this paper in which I defend *lex iniusta* from several charges brought against it by Hart, it is worth noting the context of these charges within the larger critique of natural law offered by Hart. Several of his main objections have more to do with the traditional meta-ethical foundations upon which natural lawyers have built their theories than upon anything conceptually tied to the principle of *lex iniusta* of necessity. So, for instance, he argues that the theory of natural law presupposes an outdated view of nature according to which all substances, whether rational or not, are ordered to a particular end.[19] Furthermore, he argues that even if one restricts the notion of natural teleology to rational agents, one still finds far too much disagreement among people to derive anything more than mere survival as the end of human action.[20] It is easy to see that these criticisms of natural law have little to do with the contents of *lex iniusta* and far more to do with the meta-ethical theories which natural law theorists tend to hold. Since there is nothing incoherent about a deontologist or utilitarian holding the principle of *lex iniusta*, I consider the above arguments as tangential to the main concern of this paper.

CONSTRAINTS ON THE THEORETICIAN

A general line of argument that Hart levels against natural law theory is that it is unable to give the legal theorist any new useful tools by which to analyze the law and instead clouds the theoretical field by unjustifiably restricting the area to be investigated. In this section, I will begin by looking at Hart's argument and then briefly examine whether his argument is sound. I will then turn to the issue concerning how much damage his argument does to the project of natural law.

He begins this particular attack on natural law by noting that there are two rival concepts of law that can be adopted, a broad one and a narrow one. The broad notion is the one he proposes and encompasses "all rules which are valid by formal tests of a system of primary and secondary rules."[21] Importantly, this notion encompasses all such laws regardless of their conformity to moral norms. The second notion of law, which he describes as narrow, is that which he sees as the natural lawyer's concept of law. On this view, law includes all that the broader concept includes, except those laws that violate norms of morality, or justice broadly construed.

Given these two concepts of law, he poses a question: If one were to take up the theoretic study of law as a "social phenomenon," which concept should be used to govern the range of subject matter in which the theorist works?[22] In his mind, "It seems clear that nothing is to be gained in the theoretical or scientific study of law . . . by adopting the narrower concept."[23] He does, however, think that much would be lost by adopting such an approach. He argues, quite plausibly it seems, that if one were to restrict the area of investigation to the domain governed by the narrower concept, one would completely ignore many rules which resemble laws in nearly every respect. These laws may have been formed by the same people, acting in the same official capacity, have been promulgated in the same way to the same people, and have been enforced in identical fashion. There surely seems to be, as Hart argues, an unfortunate effect of adopting the narrower domain of investigation. No one could argue against his claim that "nothing, surely, but confusion could follow from a proposal to leave the study of such rules to another discipline."[24]

It is impossible to disagree with his argument against employing the narrow concept to govern one's area of investigation. If any theorist who worked on any aspect of law completely disregarded all rules that failed to meet the strict standard of law because they acted against the common good (or were unjust in some other way), then a large and important area would be left uninvestigated. Whether he has established that his broad concept of law should be used to determine the domain of legal theory or not, he has certainly shown that the narrow concept should not be used in this fashion.

Having conceded much of the argument, let us turn to the question of how this particular critique affects natural law theorists. As Hart himself points out, no legal theorist has proposed such a restriction on the domain of investigation.[25] Since there have been many legal theorists who have adopted the theory of natural law—indeed for centuries most legal theorists adhered to this view—it seems that Hart's characterization of how natural lawyers restrict the domain of investigation is flawed. As Cristobal Orrego notes, "This fact should have led Hart to realize that the theory of natural law simply does not propose and never has proposed, a restricted concept of law in the way he understands it."[26] Perhaps Orrego goes too far here in suggesting that this fact implies something about the concept of law used by natural lawyers, but it seems to imply, at the very least, that the theory of natural law does not demand the draconian restrictions concerning the area of legal investigation that Hart contends.

The example of history, although it makes Hart's claims about natural law less plausible, does not completely rule out his conclusion concerning the subject matter of legal investigation. Hart still has the possibility of accepting the history of the theory of natural law and yet remaining firm in his contention that the theory of natural law demands such a restriction on the area of legal theory, whether natural lawyers have always realized this restriction or not. If he can show that the theory of natural law demands such a restriction, history may serve his own ends. Even natural lawyers, he could contend, have always realized the limits of legal theory should not be restricted in this fashion, and yet the theory of natural law demands such a restriction. Thus, in the end, even the intuitions of natural lawyers are incompatible with the implications of the theory of natural law.

Against such an attack, the natural lawyer has at least two possible responses. The first, suggested by Orrego, is that the traditional understanding of the subject of a science concerns the investigation of opposites, "and, in the case of law, that it was a 'science of the just and unjust.'"[27] He defends this claim historically by pointing to examples of natural lawyers who understood the bounds of legal investigation in this way[28] and conceptually by arguing that this does not destroy the principle of *lex iniusta*, but provides the important context in which it acts as a central legal principle.[29] One could also defend against Hart's attack by simply pointing out that fully legal acts, as the natural lawyer understands them, are a subspecies of a certain kind of social rules, and it is the latter, not the former, which governs legal studies. This seems fully in keeping with the history of the theory of natural law, and fully defensible. No science restricts itself to the smallest possible species it can investigate. The fact that an area of investigation is broad does not imply that there are not distinctions within that area that are crucial to its investigation. Finally, the retort that this would make legal theory primarily concerned with something other than law presupposes that unjust laws are not laws *in any sense*. This common presupposition has already been addressed.

PRACTICAL DEFICIENCIES OF THE THEORY OF NATURAL LAW

Another general line of argument Hart presents against the theory of natural law attempts to show that there are serious practical consequences of adopting such a theory. Although some critics charge that this theory brings about anarchy, he argues that, upon being educated in the theory of natural law, citizens will be less willing or able to resist inequity, thus leading not to anarchy but to a state of blind obedience. He also argues that the theory of natural law will be unable to deal critically with a variety of difficult practical situations while being mindful of various nuances of different cases. In cases concerning when to obey laws, when to allow oneself to be punished for breaking unjust laws, and what to do in situations that seem to demand breaking the principle of *nulla poena sine lege*, the natural lawyer seems to have nothing insightful to say. In this section, I will deal with each practical argument in turn, attempting to show that he fails to make conclusive judgements against the theory of natural law.

THE DANGER OF ANARCHY

The first practical danger that may be associated with a natural law theory is the danger of anarchy. The notion here is that if people are told that an unjust law is no law at all, they will fairly quickly fall into the habit of deciding that any law with which they disagree is an unjust one and thus does not demand obedience. Hart finds this worry to be a motivating factor in earlier thinkers, like Bentham and Austin, who resolutely defended a strict distinction between law and morality.[30] Hart admits that this danger "may well have been exaggerated."[31] Although he does qualify the extent of this danger, it does appear to him that there is a danger of anarchy, albeit a far smaller one than earlier thinkers predicted, which may follow widespread acceptance of the *lex iniusta* principle. It is not at all clear what gives him reason to think this. Perhaps he accepts the reasons offered by Bentham and Austin, just not their degree of concern, but since there is no textual evidence of this within the *Concept of Law*, I will refrain from examining those reasons.

What can be reasonably attributed to Hart is the claim that people will make hasty decisions, based upon their belief that a law is unjust, to disobey that law.[32] It seems that this hasty decision could take two forms and it is not clear which one Hart has in mind. On the one hand, someone might hastily decide (perhaps because of self-interest) that a law is unjust. This hasty decision, once made, reasonably leads to the decision not to obey the law. Let's describe such a decision (or series of decisions) as hasty(i). On the other hand, someone might very reasonably decide that a particular law is unjust and then hastily decide that because it is unjust, he need not obey it. Let's describe this second kind of decision (or series of decisions) as hasty(ii). Putting aside which notion Hart had in mind, is it reasonable to claim that either of these types of hasty decisions will be made if people accept the natural law theory?

Let us look first at cases where people make decisions that are hasty(i). Such cases, which amount to little more than deceptively self-justifying one's actions, cannot be completely avoided in any population, no matter what theory of law it follows. It seems perfectly likely that many people will disobey laws and convince themselves that their actions are just using the sort of reasoning as that described in the case of hasty(i). Exactly the same sort of reasoning could not be used to justify disobeying laws if one accepts a positivist theory of law rather than a natural law theory. At the same time, it seems that a parallel opportunity to decide to break the law appears within a positivist schema. According to such a schema, it is not the case that one ought to obey every law, regardless of its moral evaluation. Thus, it seems likely that many will hastily decide (perhaps because of self-interest) that something is an unjust but perfectly valid law. This hasty decision, once made, reasonably leads to the decision not to obey the law. Let's call such a decision (or series of decisions) hasty(iii). The parallels between decisions that are hasty(i) and those that are hasty(iii) are obvious. While it is true that the former can only show up when someone follows a natural law theory, it is also true that the later depends upon a positivist view.[33] Little can be gleaned from this analysis concerning which theory is more likely to provoke people to disobey laws. If anything, it seems just as likely that someone who held the natural law view would make a hasty(i) decision as that someone who held a positivist view would make a hasty(iii) decision.

Is it still plausible that people who hold a natural law theory would be uniquely susceptible to making hasty(ii) decisions? Certainly nothing said above rules out such a danger. Moreover, it seems entirely plausible that the principle of *lex iniusta* could lead to such decisions. Take for instance a statute that does not prescribe something positively immoral but merely proscribes some action that, although not morally mandatory, can in no way be connected (either by performing or refraining from performing) to the common good. At least on some versions of natural law theory, such a proscription would be unjust. It seems plausible that a citizen following the *lex iniusta* principle would have no reason to obey this unjust law; after all, it is no law at all. Yet, there is a certain danger with this utter disregard for unjust laws.

There seem to be two causes for concern here. On the one hand, such disregard for the law may lead others, especially if they do not see the reasoning behind one's disobedience, to disobey laws themselves. On the other hand, it may be the case that even though the law does not itself lead to the common good, the disobedience of the law on a particular occasion may bring about a social disruption that hurts the common good. In both cases, it seems better for the society for an individual person to obey a particular unjust law. Although it may be the case that the *lex iniusta* principle may make people believe that there is no reason whatsoever for obeying unjust laws, natural lawyers can be sensitive to this worry. Aquinas, for instance, writes that unjust "laws do not bind in conscience, except perhaps in order to avoid scandal or disturbance, for which cause a man should even yield his right."[34] Thus, the decision of whether or not one is bound to obey a particular unjust law on a particular occasion is not settled by the principle of *lex iniusta*. While it is true that someone may misuse this principle in order to do as one wishes, every other legal theory can surely be misconstrued and abused in similar ways.

THE DANGER OF INAPPROPRIATE PASSIVITY

A distinct and in many ways opposite danger is that citizens under the sway of the theory of natural law would not be ready and able to disobey the law when morality demanded that they do so.[35] Hart begins with an important question:

> In what way is it better, when faced with morally iniquitous demands, to think 'This is in no sense law' rather than 'This is law but too iniquitous to obey or apply'? Would this make men more clear-headed or readier to disobey when morality demands it?[36]

Hart answers this question himself. He notes that it "scarcely seems" that any amount of education in the theory of natural law will equip citizens with the tools to be more able to recognize unjust laws or more ready to resist them when morality demands it. Positivism, in contrast, does not fail in similar respects. What is obviously necessary to make citizens see the issues clearly, and thus be ready to resist evil, even when backed by valid laws, is a theory which preserves "the sense that the certification of something as legally valid is not conclusive of the question of obedience."[37] Putting aside for the moment the perhaps overly strict formulation by which an unjust law is "in no sense law," how is a defendant of natural law to respond to this claim? Orrego has attempted to respond to this round of Hart's objections with a threefold criticism of Hart's argument.[38] I will examine each step of Orrego's response in turn.

Orrego's first point takes Hart to task for his comment which begins "no doubt ideas have their influence, but . . ."[39] and continues to suggest that it is implausible that the ideas proposed by the theory of natural law would help make men more clear-sighted when confronted with actual cases of unjust laws.[40] Later, Hart suggests that what is precisely needed in such situations is education in the ideas of positivism. Orrego cries foul. If ideas have such a limited impact in the case of education in the natural law, the same should be the case for educating someone in any other legal theory. In this case, Orrego seems to read too much into a brief comment. Nothing in Hart's argument turns on the notion that ideas have little impact. If he did intend this as an argument against the natural law theory, then surely it works equally against all legal theories, as Orrego suggests, but nothing in Hart's argument demands such a reading. Instead, Hart seems to be noting that although ideas are important, not all ideas are equally illuminating; some, like those of the natural lawyers, merely throw dust into the air.

Orrego's second point against Hart's practical objections to the theory of natural law is not based upon a perceived double standard, as with the first, but with lack of supporting evidence. Hart's objection, in brief, is that people following a natural law theory will resist evil less than those who follow a view more in keeping with his own. Yet, Orrego argues, "Hart is in the sphere of suppositions."[41] No evidence of any kind is given for this claim.

At this point, Hart simply relies on the intuitions of the reader. It "scarcely seems" that training in the theory of natural law will help a citizen in a hard situation, while "what surely is most needed" is education in his own theory (or one which agrees with it on the broad points concerning the relationship between morality and the law).[42] Perhaps the intuitions of many readers clearly agree with those of Hart, but Orrego demands more than this. In this, Orrego surely seems correct. He contends that an historical investigation would need to be performed in order to see if there is any merit in Hart's claim. Only an investigation examining the actual practices of citizens who held different legal theories could resolve this issue.[43] In any case, it seems that Hart's argument here rests on too thin a foundation to be taken seriously.

As a third point, Orrego contends that Hart's criticism must be leveled equally against natural lawyers and any system which includes a particular moral criterion within its conditions for validity.[44] Orrego points out that Hart not only allows for this possibility, but even admits that the United States is an example of such a system.[45] In Orrego's view, the citizens of the United States should then be held up as an example which can be analyzed to test Hart's contention. He asks: "Has the American's [sic] belief that no positive law can be valid if it violates the right to freedom of speech . . . made them more resistant or less resistant to laws that seem to violate such [a] right?"[46] Orrego concludes, on the basis of the well-known resistance of Americans to laws which violate their freedom of speech, that "subordination of law to morals increases the possibilities of resistance."[47] In this strong conclusion, I must disagree with Orrego. In order for this example to be used legitimately as a test case, one must be able to show that the resistance which Americans have shown to laws that violate this right flows from purely moral motives. In other words, one must show that Americans resist these laws purely because they conflict with a moral standard to which all laws must confirm. In point of fact, however, laws that violate freedom of speech often meet resistance because they violate a legal and constitutional right rather than a moral one. If

Americans had historically shown overwhelming resistance to a kind of law because it violated a moral right, even in the absence of a corresponding legal right, then perhaps one could conclude as Orrego does.

Even if one grants him his contention that the natural law's subordination of legal validity to morality is similar to the United States' subordination of legal validity to morality on the issue of certain freedoms, there is still too little information to conclude as he does. Whatever resistance commonly arises in the United States upon the enactment of a new law that violates certain rights, it is not at all clear that the reason for such strong resistance is the belief that no law can be valid if it violates certain basic freedoms. Resistance may owe far more to the national character of self-reliance and self-determination, or upon many other factors that weigh neither in favor of nor against Hart's thesis. To show that "recognition of the subordination of law to morals"[48] increases the chances of resistance, as Orrego contends, or diminishes such chances, as Hart contends, is a far more difficult task than either seems willing to admit.

Hart concludes his brief discussion of this negative effect of the theory of natural law with something approaching an argument. He writes:

> This sense, that there is something outside the official system, by reference to which in the last resort the individual must solve his problems of obedience, is surely more likely to be kept alive among those who are accustomed to think that rules of law may be iniquitous, than among those who think that nothing iniquitous can anywhere have the status of law.[49]

As phrased, it appears to have the character of dialectic argument. However, when examined, his claim seems to be able to establish quite conclusively that those who employ only a narrow concept of law will be unable to reflect upon the possibility that laws may be iniquitous. Consider the following formalization, built upon (rather than strictly extracted from) Hart's 'argument':

(1) Those who employ the narrow concept of law consider all laws to be just.

(2) Those who employ the broad concept of law do not consider all laws to be just.

(3) Some laws are unjust.

(4) One has reason to test laws according to some external rule if and only if one does not consider all laws to be just.

(5) Those who employ the narrow concept of law consider unjust laws to be just. (By 1 and 3).

(6) Those who employ the narrow concept of law have no reason to test laws according to some external rule. (By 1 and 4).

(7) Those who employ the narrow concept of law consider unjust laws to be just and have no reason to test them according to some external rule. (By 5 and 6).

(8) Those who employ the broad concept of law have reason to test unjust laws according to some external rule. (By 2 and 4).[50]

Proposition 7, which appears to be devastating to the natural law theory, seems to follow from premises to which, Hart suggests, natural lawyers are committed. The argument employed to reach this conclusion, however, if leveled at the natural lawyer, is "flagrantly fallacious."[51] The problem any natural lawyer should have with this argument is that, although each premise seems independently reasonable, different premises use the term 'law' with different meanings.[52] Thus, in 1 the meaning of 'law' is taken to include the full character of law, which includes conformity to morality.[53] In 3, however, "law" is taken to include (among other things) all statutes enacted by a government.[54] Thus, in order for the argument to bring about any conclusion whatsoever, one must overlook the equivocation of "law."

Perhaps, however, this argument reveals a danger inherent within the theory of natural law itself. Does the existence of this fallacious argument show just how difficult it is to navigate the terminological labyrinth of the natural law theory? Since it employs various senses of the term 'law,' perhaps this theory is doomed to cause confusion in the minds of those faced with difficult decisions concerning civil obedience. I see no reason to think this is the case. When spoken of in the abstract, the senses of law can become confusing, but in a concrete situation, it seems unlikely for someone to conclude that just because a certain command seems to be a law that it must be law in the most complete sense and thus be in accord with justice.

THE DANGER OF OVERSIMPLIFYING MORAL ISSUES

After discussing both the dangers of anarchy and mindless submission, Hart turns to what he considers an even stronger reason to prefer a theory which employs a broader concept of law. This reason is that natural law theories, which employ the narrow concept of law, "may grossly oversimplify the variety of moral issues to which [unjust laws] give rise."[55] He briefly suggests three possible problems which may be mishandled by such a theory: the problem of whether or not to obey unjust laws, the problem of when to submit to punishment for breaking unjust laws, and the problem of how to punish people who obeyed laws that commanded grossly immoral acts. I will turn to each of these problems in turn. Since Hart does not dwell at length upon the reasons why natural lawyers will be unable to handle each case, I will only briefly indicate the ways in which a natural lawyer may handle different situations while remaining sensitive to the complexities to which unjust laws give rise.

The first question, concerning whether one should obey an unjust law or not, has already been discussed above, but it is worth returning to it briefly. It is simply not the case that any natural law theorist must ultimately think that unjust laws lack motivating power entirely. Aquinas, one of only several natural law theorists that Hart mentions, is strongly committed to the view that sometimes unjust laws ought to be respected out of concern for the order necessary for the common good.[56] Moreover, this view enables the reasons for performing an action in keeping with an unjust law to become clear. Unlike obeying many just laws, the force motivating obedience to unjust laws comes from the wish to avoid negative consequences resulting from other citizens' perceptions of one's action, not from the utility of the law itself, nor from respect for the authority from which it originated.

The second problem that Hart suggests may be maltreated from within a natural law perspective concerns submission to punishment, not obedience. He does not specifically address why he thinks the natural lawyer could not respond to this kind of moral dilemma. He simply states, "There is Socrates' question of submission: Am I to submit to punishment for disobedience or make my escape?"[57] He later notes, when speaking in general terms, that following a natural law approach "may blind us" from seeing the "complexity and variety" of different issues.[58] The idea behind his criticism seems to be this: If one accepts the view that an unjust law is no law at all, then different cases concerning disobedience to unjust laws flatten out. In answer to the question: "Should one submit to punishment for breaking an unjust law," one can only respond by denying that any law was broken. Thus the question becomes: "Should one submit to punishment without having broken any law?" This latter question, however, seems to cloud rather than clarify the issue that is actually at stake. Surely the case of Socrates is different than it would have been if he had been sentenced to death without being accused of breaking any law whatsoever.

The natural lawyer, however, can respond to this charge. Although the response, as well as the way in which Socrates' dilemma is solved, will depend upon the specific accounts of law and morality that are available to the natural law theorist, one particular response to Hart stands out. Natural lawyers, even those who take a hard line interpretation of the *lex iniusta* principle, can respond that they still are able to distinguish unjust laws (even if the use of the term 'law' is actually equivocal) from the complete absence of commands entirely.[59] Just because they are unwilling to grant the status of law to such unjust statutes does not mean they are incapable of describing such things in other meaningful ways. To return again to Aquinas, one can see that he is sensitive to the category of unjust laws, and even maintains that they sometimes bind in conscience.[60] Although no systematic treatment of Socrates' dilemma can be made here, it certainly seems open to the natural lawyer to propose that in situations in which one is bound in conscience to obey unjust laws, one ought to submit to punishment, while in other cases one need not do so.[61]

Finally, Hart suggests that natural lawyers would be unable to address the problems that arose in the aftermath of World War II in an intelligent and enlightening way. The question "Are we to punish those who did evil things when they were permitted by evil rules then in force?"[62] seems to resist a clear treatment for the same reason that the Socrates dilemma resisted intelligent treatment. The phrase "permitted by evil rules then in force" loses meaning if there is no category of unjust laws. As shown above, however, there is no reason to think that there is no distinct category for unjust laws within a natural law framework; instead, they simply resist placing these rules within the same category as just laws.

Hart also suggests another reason that this question will not be clarified, but instead clouded, by a natural law response. In his mind, the immediate natural law response would be that these men broke the natural law and thus they can be punished. No recourse to the positive law in force at the time of the crime is needed.[63] The common interpretation of the principle of *nulla poena sine lege* is thus rendered useless on a natural law reading.[64] But of course, this suggested response would entail that a state may punish any offense against the natural law, a claim that few if any natural law theorists would accept. There is nothing within the theory of natural law that requires one to reject the acceptance of the common interpretation of the *nulla poena* principle. This is not to say that an answer to problems like those facing post-war courts is easily available to the natural lawyer. Instead, such problems remain difficult and in need of careful treatment, yet they are no more difficult than they are for those who, like Hart, reject the theory of natural law.

In the end, my analysis of the natural law has been a modest one. I have not defended it against every attack that has been leveled against it, nor have I tried to provide solid reasons for accepting it. Even when addressing the theoretical and practical consequences of accepting such a theory, I have merely defended it against charges of inadequacy; I have not provided any positive benefits to adopting such a view of law. I hope to have shown, however, the inadequacy of several of Hart's objections to the principle of *lex iniusta non est lex*.

NOTES

1. Plato, *Laws*, trans. Trevor J. Saunders, in *Plato: Complete Works*, ed. John M. Cooper (Indianapolis: Hackett Publishing Co., 1997), IV, 715b.
2. Cicero, *On the Laws*, trans. K. Ziegler in *On the Commonwealth and On the Laws*, ed. J. Zetzel (Cambridge: Cambridge University Press, 1999), II, v, 11.
3. H. L. A. Hart, *The Concept of Law*, 2nd ed (Oxford: Clarendon Press, 1994), 156.
4. Augustine, *On Free Choice of the Will*, trans. Thomas Williams (Indianapolis: Hackett Publishing Co., 1993), I v 11.
5. For debate over the force of the statement, see John Finnis, *Natural Law and Natural Rights* (Oxford: Clarendon Press, 1980), 363: Augustine "makes one of his characters say, rather breezily, 'a law that was unjust wouldn't seem to be law.'" Against this, note Norman Kretzmann, "*Lex Iniusta Non Est Lex*: Laws on Trial in Aquinas' Court of Conscience" *American Journal of Jurisprudence* 33 (1988) 99, 101: "Notice that [Finnis's] translation is debatable, that the character into whose mouth the speech is put is also the author of the dialogue, and that 'rather breezily' is an exaggeration."
6. Aquinas, I-II, *Summa Theologiae*, trans. Fathers of the English Dominican Province (London: Burns, Oates, & Washbourne, 1920), I-II, q. 96, a. 4.
7. Hart, 156.
8. Edward Damich thinks the omission of "seems to be" is important. See "The Essence of Law According to Thomas Aquinas," *American Journal of Jurisprudence* 30 (1985) 79. Kretzmann disagrees. He writes, "It is a mistake to rest such a thesis on an emphasized English word that picks up only one ordinary sense of the Latin word 'videtur,' which can (and in the Augustine passage pretty clearly does) also have the sense of the English phrase 'is evidently.'" Kretzmann, 101-102, n. 6.
9. I do not mean that this is uniquely Hart's creation. This simple formulation, although not found in Augustine or Aquinas, has a long tradition behind it.
10. Hart, 8.
11. Such a claim seems to be put forth by Arthur Danto. See "Human Nature and Natural Law" in *Law and Philosophy: A Symposium*, ed. Sidney Hook (New York: New York University Press, 1964), 187-188.

12. Although there are differences between the two theories, both Damich and Kretzmann offer this general kind of interpretation of Aquinas's theory of natural law. See Damich, 79-96 and Kretzmann, 99-122. Mark Murphy defends what he calls the "weak natural law thesis," which is quite similar to what I call the weak reading of this principle. See *Natural Law in Jurisprudence and Politics* (Cambridge: Cambridge University Press, 2006), chapters 1–2. He does not, however, identify this weak thesis with *lex iniusta*, which he links with what he calls the strong natural law thesis. The strong natural law thesis as he formulates it is substantively the same as the first interpretation of *lex iniusta* described above.

13. John Gardner, "Nearly Natural Law," *American Journal of Jurisprudence* 52 (2007) 1, 13-14.

14. Ibid., 16.

15. Gardner's explanation asks us to imagine a person in a permanent vegetable state. Why is this person's condition a matter for concern? We do not concern ourselves over vegetables being in a similar state. The reason is because there is a central aspect of human nature that this person is lacking. In short, there is a human being who is lacking some important element that she ought to have *because of her nature*. Unjust laws ought to be thought about along these lines. An unjust law is something that is missing an important feature that it ought to have *because of the very nature of law*.

16. This is not to say, however, that the very formulation of *lex iniusta* is contradictory. See Murphy, 13, for a defense of the view that "it is not always self-contradictory to make assertions of the form "a—X is not an X."

17. Hart, 209.

18. For defenses against the claim concerning violation of language, see Damich, 79-96, Kretzmann, 99-122, and, in his own way, J.S. Russell, "Trial By Slogan: Natural Law and *Lex Iniusta Non Est Lex*," *Law and Philosophy* 19 (2000) 433-449.

19. Hart, 186.

20. Ibid., 191-192.

21. Ibid., 209.

22. Ibid.

23. Ibid.

24. Ibid.

25. Ibid.

26. Orrego, Cristobal, "H.L.A. Hart's Arguments against Classical Natural Law Theory," *American Journal of Jurisprudence* 48 *(2003)* 297, 316-317.

27. Ibid., 317.

28. Ibid., n. 47.

29. Ibid.

30. Hart, 211.

31. Ibid.

32. Ibid.

33. To be precise, decisions that are hasty(iii) could develop within someone who held any legal theory, positivist or otherwise, that did not demand obedience to valid but unjust laws.

34. Aquinas, *Summa Theologiae*, I-II, q. 96, a. 4.

35. Hart, 210-211.

36. Ibid., 210.

37. Ibid.
38. Orrego, 318-319.
39. Hart, 210.
40. Orrego, 318.
41. Ibid.
42. Hart, 210.
43. Perhaps Orrego is too optimistic when he notes that an historical investigation could resolve this issue. To resolve this issue truly, one would need to perform a large scale study of numerous individuals who had relevantly similar moral behaviors and intellectual capacities. Although their adherence to legal theories would need to be different, many other factors, including the various particulars of given circumstances, would need to be closely connected. It seems unlikely that history could provide clear examples by which to collect the data needed. One might attempt to perform some investigation along the lines of recent work in experimental philosophy, but even then it would be difficult to know if the legal theories held by certain individuals influenced their decisions regarding civil disobedience, or if their general attitude to social authority influenced (or predisposed them to) a given legal theory.
44. Orrego, 319.
45. Orrego points to a passage from "Positivism and the Separation of Law and Morals" for support. See Hart, "Positivism and the Separation of Law and Morals," *Harvard Law Review* 71 (1958) 593, 599-600.
46. Orrego, 319.
47. Ibid.
48. Ibid.
49. Hart, 210.
50. I do not mean to imply that someone employing such a concept will be able to pick out which laws are unjust, then test those laws against some external rule. I merely mean that such a person will have reason to test all laws, including those that will later be revealed as unjust, according to such a rule.
51. Orrego, 320. Orrego formalizes this argument in a different manner, but there is no substantive disagreement between our interpretations of Hart's argument.
52. Another option available to natural lawyers is to deny 3. They could explain that there are no unjust laws, but rather only things that are both unjust and appear to have the character of law.
53. In order to avoid gross misunderstanding, it is vital to note that this conformity does not mean that the laws of a particular government need to blindly repeat what morality dictates. Instead, it is sufficient for laws to be aimed at the common good and avoid conflict with what morality commands.
54. Or at least those statutes that are valid according to the society's particular conditions for validity.
55. Hart, 211.
56. Aquinas, I-II, q. 96, a. 4.
57. Hart, 211.
58. Ibid.
59. They are similarly able to distinguish them from commands that fail to meet the criterion of law in other ways, for instance, if they originate from ordinary citizens rather than from someone charged with care of the community.
60. Aquinas, I-II, q. 94, a. 6.

61. I do not endorse or defend this view, but merely mean to show how one may bring some subtlety to the Socrates problem from within a natural law framework. Since subtle treatments concerning unjust laws can be made, and indeed have been made as is clear in the case of Aquinas, one need not accept the simplistic reading of Hart, whereby the natural lawyer simply makes a "refusal, made once and for all, to recognize evil laws as valid for any purpose." Hart, 211.

62. Ibid.

63. Ibid., 211-212.

64. Orrego suggests a different response than the one I am giving. He argues that there is no reason why a natural lawyer must try to accommodate what I am calling the common interpretation and he calls the "legal positivist conception" of *nulla poena*. This understanding of the principle maintains that it is not just for a state to punish a citizen for committing an act that was not outlawed by positive law at the time the act was performed. Orrego contends, "In my view, it is inconsistent to ascribe to natural law theory simultaneously a 'natural law' concept of law and a "legal positivist' conception of the *nulla poena* principle." Orrego, 323. I cannot agree with this sentiment. As I see it, the force of Hart's objection relies on the intuitive force of the common interpretation of this principle. This force remains whatever conception of law one has. Thus, to respond to Hart's objection one must show either that the natural lawyer can accommodate this principle as well as the positivist, or else spell out the grounds on which one rejects the common interpretation of the principle. Merely asserting that the sense of *"lege"* should be anything whatsoever contained within the law of morality does nothing by which to nullify the intuitive validity of the common interpretation of *nulla poena*.

THE NATURAL LAW, THE VIRTUES, AND CONSEQUENCES IN THE ETHICAL THEORY OF SAINT THOMAS AQUINAS

David J. Klassen

What follows is an introduction to Thomas Aquinas' understanding of the natural law as the foundation of rational ethics, with reference to the texts of Aquinas himself. After discussing the natural law, I shall consider how it is related to Aquinas' teaching on the virtues. Finally, I shall examine the question as to whether Aquinas' ethics might be described as deontological, teleological or consequentialist. The aim of this essay is not to give a full account of Aquinas' moral philosophy, but rather to give an idea of its basic contours and to try to clear up some common misunderstandings. I am proposing that Aquinas' ethical theory does not fit neatly into any of the categories of contemporary ethics. It is a more comprehensive ethical theory that transcends those categories.

Aquinas' teaching as to the content of the natural law will be treated in more detail later in the context of a discussion of how it is known. But let us begin with a quick summary. The natural law in its strict sense consists of (1) the most general precept, that good shall be done and pursued and evil avoided; (2) precepts of love of God and love of neighbor; and (3) precepts identifying basic goods to be pursued, such as life, knowledge and education of children. These precepts of the natural law, also called its first principles, are the starting-points for all our moral deliberations.

THE NATURAL LAW AND HUMAN REASON

Aquinas begins his "Treatise on Law," comprising questions 90-108 of the first part of the second part of the *Summa Theologiae* (*ST* I-II, qq. 90-108), by defining law as "a rule and measure of acts" and as "something pertaining to reason."[1] Nevertheless, many contemporary interpreters of his theory of the natural law lose sight of the place of reason. They mistakenly think that Aquinas derives precepts of the natural law from observation of pre-rational inclinations, tendencies or urges including those associated with procreation, affection for others and the desire to do good. In fact, such inclinations do not teach us the natural law. Rather, it is the natural law, consisting of ordinances of reason, which teaches us when those inclinations are natural in the sense of being in accord with human nature and when they are not. Since humans are rational animals, only those inclinations that are in accord with reason (i.e. in conformity with the natural law) are in accord with human nature. Vicious or corrupt inclinations may be "from nature," but they are not natural in the sense of being in accord with human nature insofar as it is specified by reason.[2]

Unlike irrational animals, humans are not guided solely by instinct and appetite. The human intellect apprehends the natural law as the rule and measure of our free actions. Humans may freely choose to follow or to disregard the natural law, which is defined as "the rational creature's participation in the eternal law" (the eternal law is the law in the mind of God).[3] Non-rational creatures are also said to be guided by Eternal Reason in following their instincts or inclinations, but since they do not partake in it as rational or intellectual creatures, they are not guided by "law" in its proper sense, that is, something that is rationally understood and freely accepted.[4]

FIRST PRINCIPLES OF THE NATURAL LAW

The most basic moral principles are the first principles of the natural law. They are also called the first principles of practical reason, the first principles of action and, in *ST* I-II, q. 94, a. 2, the precepts of the natural law. In its strictest sense, the natural law is nothing other than its first principles, for any conclusions drawn from the first principles are said by Aquinas to belong to human law as distinct from natural law (*ST* I-II, q. 95, a. 2). In a less strict sense, the natural law also includes "certain secondary and more detailed precepts, which are, as it were, conclusions following closely from first principles" (*ST* I-II, q. 94, a. 6).

The way in which the first principles become known to us, and question of which propositions may be counted as first principles of the natural law, are topics of considerable debate among contemporary interpreters of Aquinas' ethics. The interpreters may be classified into four main groups.[5] The first group includes those previously mentioned, who maintain that human reason is guided and directed by observation of pre-rational or sub-rational inclinations, such as affective and volitional inclinations, in attaining to knowledge of the natural law.[6] A second group consists of those who maintain that according to Aquinas the precepts of the natural law are rationally derived from prior theoretical knowledge, such as from principles of metaphysics or from observation of human nature or human behavior.[7] A third group emphasizes Aquinas' texts which say that the first precepts or principles of the natural law are *per se nota* (self-evident) and indemonstrable. Members of the third group say that the precepts are known through a direct insight of reason that is preceded by the experience of an inclination which supplies background data for the insight, but deny there is an inference of "ought" from "is," i.e. of a precept of law from an affective or appetitive inclination or from any theoretical or metaphysical proposition.[8] None of the three groups just mentioned accepts a literal interpretation of Aquinas' texts which say that the first principles of the natural law are innate or implanted by God or nature in human reason,[9] although other commentators, who might be considered as a fourth group, have taken those texts at face value.[10] In the rest of this section, I offer a brief account of human knowledge of first principles of the natural law according to the fourth type of interpretation, having regard to Aquinas' texts which treat them as innate and "habitually known," becoming self-evident to human reason through operation of a "natural habit" called *synderesis*.[11]

Aquinas says that the first principles of the natural law are self-evident[12] and instilled in the human mind by God or nature.[13] We are born with these as part of our natural equipment as human beings. However, although the natural law is already present in infants, infants cannot yet act according to the natural law. The natural law is said to be only habitually present in infants, which means that infants are not yet aware of it and do not consider it.[14] We only become actually aware of the precepts of the natural law when we reach the age of reason. The precepts become actually known to us, which means that we become aware of them and consider them, by the operation of a natural habit called *synderesis*.[15] Synderesis is triggered in situations of morally-relevant experience.[16]

Our initial awareness of the natural law may be described as implicit knowledge. That is, the precepts may not be explicitly stated as they would be by a moral philosopher. When making moral decisions based on them, we do not normally explicitly state general principles such as "it is wrong to do evil to other people," although we assume such principles. For example, when we realize that a specific act of torture is wrong, we have implicitly reasoned from more general principles, such as "it is wrong to do evil to others." If asked why this particular act is wrong, we would say it is wrong because it is torture. If asked why torture is wrong, we would say that it is wrong because it is wrong to hurt or do evil to others, and that torture involves hurting others. The precepts of the natural law are at the basis of any understanding that some actions are good and just and other actions are not. However, in order to explicitly identify the first principles, we would have to analyze our moral reasoning to determine its most basic and general presuppositions.[17]

The most general of the first principles, "the first precept of law" upon which all the others are founded, is that good shall be done and pursued and evil avoided.[18] However, this is only a statement of the common theme of the natural law, and does not tell us what things are good. We need more specific precepts to guide us.

Thomas in fact says that there are many (*multa*) first principles or precepts of the natural law, although they have a common foundation in the single first precept of law.[19] The others include more specific precepts that we employ in moral decision-making. Like the first precept of law, these other first principles of the natural law are self-evident.[20] They do not need to be derived as conclusions by reasoning from the first precept. Inasmuch as they are self-evident or *per se nota* (literally, "known through themselves"), we know them by a kind of intellectual intuition. We know all first principles—including those of the natural law *and* those of speculative reason such as the principle of non-contradiction—by a simple act of knowing which Aquinas calls understanding.[21] The simple act of understanding first principles is a kind of intellectual "seeing" or vision.[22] It differs from discursive reasoning which moves from one thing to another, such as moving by logical inference from principles to conclusions.[23] We can prove things which are discursively derived as conclusions from premises, but we cannot "prove" the simply-known first principles, which are the starting-points for all proofs. We *just know* them with a simple act of insight which is the final court of appeal for all knowledge.[24]

The fact that the first principles of the natural law are self-evident and that our knowledge of them is not derived by inference from observation of other facts about nature, or from prior metaphysical or speculative principles, provides an answer to one of the most common criticisms of the natural law: that it involves an illicit inference from an "is" to an "ought." Those who do not understand Aquinas' natural law theory often say that he makes an inference from descriptive propositions about nature ("is" propositions) to prescriptive propositions which tell us what we should do ("ought" propositions). If such an inference is made, it is illicit, because the conclusion of the inference contains something—the "ought"—that is not contained in the premises. However, Aquinas never makes such an inference. He realizes that practical reason, which tells us what we ought to do, must have its very own starting-points which are self-evident and not inferred from the "is" propositions of speculative reason. These starting-points are the first principles of the natural law, also called the first practical principles. Hence, he says that, "it is clear that, as the speculative reason argues about speculative things, so that practical reason argues about practical things. Therefore we must have, implanted in us by nature, not only speculative principles, but also practical principles."[25]

The most important of the precepts of the natural law are the precepts of love, which command us to love God wholeheartedly and to love our neighbours as ourselves.[26] There are different levels of understanding of the precepts of love. In other words, some people may have a very limited understanding of them, and others may have a more complete understanding. For example, those who do not believe in God the creator still have some general and confused conception of God, which is whatever they consider as the greatest good or greatest source of happiness.[27] Therefore, the precept commanding love of God applies to everyone, although Aquinas would say that it is most fully understood by those who believe in the God of Christian theism.

Thomas says in *ST* I-II, q. 94, a. 2 that there is an inclination according to the nature of our reason to know the truth about God. This inclination is related to love of God, since Aquinas follows Augustine in saying that we cannot love what we do not know.[28] Hence, the precept commanding love of God also implies that we are to seek knowledge of God. The precept associated with knowledge of God can be stated more generally as a precept that tells us to seek knowledge of the good, or as negatively stated in q. 94, a. 2, that we are "to shun ignorance." Similarly, we read in q. 94, a. 2 that there is a precept directing one "to avoid offending those among whom one has to live," which is a minimal formulation or most basic level of understanding of the love of neighbour precept.

In addition to the "first precept of law" and the precepts of love, there are additional first principles which direct us to basic goods. Reason identifies certain things as goods for the person, which we ought to seek for ourselves and for others. These goods include such things as life or survival, family life, and knowledge, which belong to "natural inclinations." In q. 94, a. 2, Thomas says that "the order of the precepts of the natural law is according to the order of the natural inclinations." He speaks of three types of inclinations: (1) those we have in common with all substances (such as the inclination to self-preservation); (2) those we have in common with other animals, such as inclinations to the union of male and female (*coniunctio maris et feminae,* sometimes translated as "sexual intercourse") and to education of offspring; and (3) those proper to man, which are according to the nature of reason, and which include the precepts of love and the precept to seek knowledge of God and to shun ignorance. Aquinas does not limit the natural law to those goods or ends specifically mentioned in q. 94, a. 2. The goods which the decalogue recognizes, such as property in the commandment not to steal, are also goods to which we are directed by precepts of the natural law.

NATURAL INCLINATIONS

Probably the most misunderstood part of Aquinas' teaching on the natural law is his teaching on the natural inclinations. It is often assumed, even by some eminent Thomists, that the natural inclinations Aquinas speaks of are feelings, desires or urges which provide us with basic data which inform us of the content of the natural law. But if that is so, how could the natural law be what Aquinas calls "law," which is an ordinance of reason? How would we be any different from other animals, who just follow their urges and instincts? James E. White points out several problems with this understanding of natural law. For example, he says that, "Male animals have a natural tendency to be aggressive and to dominate females, but are these tendencies good?"[29] The Thomistic natural law theory has fallen into disrepute inasmuch as some people have mistakenly thought that it tells us to blindly follow our urges and desires, which we know are not always good. In addition, if we were to infer the prescriptions of the natural law from descriptions of our non-rational inclinations, we would be making an illicit inference from "is" to "ought," as discussed above.

Indeed, Thomas does say in q. 94, a. 2 that "all those things to which man has a natural inclination are naturally apprehended by reason as being good, and consequently as objects of pursuit, and their contraries as evil, and objects of avoidance." However, this statement must be understood in the context of what Thomas means by a "natural inclination." For a human being, no inclination is "natural" unless it belongs to *reason itself* (as with the inclination according to the nature of reason mentioned in q. 94, a. 2) or is naturally apprehended *by reason* as being good. In other words, to be a "natural inclination," it must belong to reason or conform with reason. A little earlier in the I-II of the *Summa theologiae,* Thomas defines what is natural to man as being in accord with reason:

> Now man derives his species from his rational soul: and consequently whatever is contrary to the order of reason is, properly speaking, contrary to the nature of man, as man; while whatever is in accord with reason, is in accord with the nature of man, as man. Now "man's good is to be in accord with reason, and his evil is to be against reason," as Dionysius states (Div. Nom. iv). Therefore human virtue, which makes a man good, and his work good, is in accord with man's nature, for as much as it accords with his reason: while vice is contrary to man's nature, in so far as it is contrary to the order of reason. (*ST* I-II, q. 71, a. 2).

Thus, not all of our inclinations are "natural" in the sense that they are virtuous and belong to the natural law. Indeed, Thomas says that, "the presence of vices and sins in man is owing to the fact that he follows the inclination of his sensitive nature against the order of his reason" (q. 71, a. 2, ad 3). The inclinations of our sensitive nature are *from nature*, but they are not always *in accord with human nature*;[30] they are not considered "natural inclinations" unless they comply with the order of reason expressed in the natural law. There is, according to St. Thomas, such a thing as knowledge by which man is ordered to an end connatural to him through a natural inclination. But that inclination is first and foremost the inclination of *reason itself,* where reason is said to contain the first and universal principles of the natural law.[31]

To sum up: the natural law consists of ordinances of reason which guide us in determining which inclinations are good and natural and which inclinations are not. Although urges and desires may be present when we apprehend the natural law, they do not inform reason of the content of the natural law. It is the reverse: human reason innately contains the guiding principles of the natural law by which we know that certain inclinations of non-rational faculties, including some belonging to our sensitive nature, are natural to humanity as being in accord with reason, and others (such as overly aggressive tendencies) are not. If we bring all of our inclinations into conformity with the order of reason, that is, into conformity with the natural law, Thomas would say that we attain a state of moral virtue, which is discussed in more detail below.

DERIVATION OF HUMAN LAW FROM THE NATURAL LAW

So far, we have looked at the natural law in its strictest sense, inasmuch as it is limited to the self-evident first principles of practical reason, also called the precepts of the natural law. Beginning from those first principles of the natural law, we can derive what Aquinas calls human law.

In *ST* I-II, q. 95, a. 2, Aquinas discusses what he means by human law. He says that, "every human law has just so much of the nature of law, as it is derived from the law of nature. But if in any point it deflects from the law of nature, it is no longer a law but a perversion of law." Then, in the same article, he describes the ways in which human law is derived from the natural law.[32] The most important point he makes is that there are two ways of deriving human law from the natural law. The first way is by logical inference that begins from first principles of the natural law (e.g. "one should do evil to no human") and arrives at conclusions (e.g. "one must not murder"). Those conclusions, inasmuch as they are logically entailed by the natural law, gain their force from the natural law. The second way, the mode of determination, is more of an art form than an exercise in logic. For example, it may be a logical conclusion derived according to the first mode that highways should be designed so that cars do not collide head-on resulting in fatalities. But it is a matter of determination, derived according to the second way and proper to the human law alone, as to whether cars should travel in the left lane or the right lane. Either determination would be compatible with the natural law.

ARE THERE EXCEPTIONS TO THE NATURAL LAW? QUESTIONS OF HISTORICAL AND CULTURAL DIVERSITY

There are no exceptions to the natural law in its first principles, but there are exceptions to the conclusions, also called secondary precepts, which make up the human law. Moreover, there is a hierarchy among the first principles or precepts of the natural law that name goods that are to be pursued, such as life and property. While property is always a good and it is always wrong to steal another's property, life is a more important good than property. Thus, according to Aquinas, it is not stealing to take another's property if the need is urgent and manifest and there is no other way to save a life.[33] The general criterion for prioritizing and choosing among the basic goods, which are ends of human action, is their ordination as means to the ultimate end (*ST* I-II, q. 13, a. 3, ad 2), which I will discuss in considering Aquinas' teleology.

While the first principles of the natural law (e.g. "avoid harming others," or "preservation of life is a good to be pursued") are said to be exceptionless norms habitually known to everyone, the secondary precepts which are derived as conclusions from the natural law, especially the more remote conclusions, are not known to everyone and admit of exceptions. Only those who possess moral and intellectual virtue will know the right answers to the most difficult moral questions, and the more one descends to matters of detail by a complex process of reasoning, the more likely it is that there are exceptions to the conclusions derived from the first principles.

Aquinas discusses the question of exceptions to the natural law in *ST* I-II, q. 94, a. 4, where he asks "Whether the natural law is the same in all men?"[34]

Inasmuch as it acknowledges limitations of human knowledge and legitimate exceptions to the secondary precepts, Aquinas' natural law theory is capable of explaining historical development. For example, it can account for the case of a cultural tradition that progressively becomes more aware of the secondary precepts (e.g. slavery is wrong), of their application in more detailed matters, and of the legitimate exceptions to those secondary precepts. It can also account for cultural variation, because it recognizes, as we read in q. 94, a. 4, that practical reason is "busied with contingent matters," and thus that different situations may arise that call for different solutions. "The general principles of the natural law," Aquinas tells us, "cannot be applied to all men in the same way on account of the great variety of human affairs: and hence arises the diversity of positive laws among various people" (*ST* I-II, q. 95, a. 2, ad 3). Cultural diversity can also be explained in virtue of the fact that Aquinas recognizes that not all peoples are equally cognizant of the secondary precepts or of their proper application in particular circumstances. In *ST* I-II, q. 94, a. 4, he gives the example of theft not being reputed to be wrong among the Germans of antiquity.[35] His explanation for their lack of knowledge is that in some the reason is perverted by passion, or evil habit, or an evil disposition of nature.

This passage ought to be read in light of another text where Aquinas gives a more complete account of how passions can overcome reason. Two of the most important distinctions made in that article are (1) between knowledge of general principles and knowledge of their application in particular cases, and (2) between knowing something habitually and considering it actually. Aquinas says,

> It may happen, then, that a man has some knowledge in general, e.g. that no fornication is lawful, and yet he does not know in particular that this act, which is fornication, must not be done; and this suffices for the will not to

> follow the universal knowledge of the reason. Again, it must be observed that nothing prevents a thing which is known habitually from not being considered actually: so that it is possible for a man to have correct knowledge not only in general but also in particular, and yet not to consider his knowledge actually: and in such a case it does not seem difficult for a man to act counter to what he does not actually consider. (*ST* I-II, q. 77, a. 2).

Therefore, Aquinas need not be taken to say in *ST* I-II, q. 94, a. 4 that the Germans lacked a general and habitual knowledge of the precept that it is wrong to steal. Rather, as one commentator has proposed, it may be that their knowledge failed in regard to application of the precept in particular cases, such as in regard to other peoples,[36] or it may be that there was a failure of their knowledge in the sense that they did not consider actually what they knew habitually when they did not consider theft to be wrong. In these ways as well, Aquinas' theory is able to explain historical and cultural variation while still maintaining that there are general principles of the natural law known to all.

NATURAL LAW AND THE VIRTUES

In contemporary ethical theory, a distinction is often made between ethics based upon the natural law and virtue ethics. Virtue ethics rightly emphasize the importance of character and the inner state of the person, and focus on the sort of person each of us ought to become. Thus, virtue ethics are in contrast to deontic systems which are concerned with assessing our external actions.[37] In its purest or most exaggerated form, virtue ethics may be thought to dispense with the need for the normative principles such as those based upon the natural law, and even to do away with the need to speak of rights and duties. Instead, the virtuous individual is held up as the norm, and one need only ask what a *virtuoso* such as Jesus or Gandhi would do in a particular situation.[38] A problem with this pure form of virtue ethics is that it begs the question of how we determine who is a virtuous individual. If we are to avoid relativism, there must be some objective and not merely arbitrary criterion by which we may determine what is and is not virtuous character and virtuous conduct.

In Aquinas' ethical theory, the virtues occupy a central place, but it is impossible to speak of them without at least implicitly speaking of first principles of practical reason (also known as precepts of the natural law) which direct us to action, and first principles of speculative reason which is concerned with knowledge for its own sake.

One way in which Aquinas defines virtue is as a habit that is a certain perfection of a power (*ST* I-II, q. 55, a. 1). There are two types of natural (as distinct from supernatural) virtues: intellectual virtues, which are virtues of right thinking that perfect human reason, and moral virtues, which are virtues of right desire and right action that perfect the appetites which motivate us to act (*ST* I-II, q. 58, aa. 1-3). Aquinas says that the first principles of speculative reason are the seeds or nurseries of intellectual virtues, and that the first principles of action, i.e. of the natural law, are the seeds of the moral virtues.[39]

What Aquinas calls the natural moral virtues perfect both the will (the "rational appetite") and the affective or sensitive appetites, whose operations are called passions (*ST* I-II, q. 59, a. 4-5). When Aquinas speaks of passions and of the operations of sensitive appetites, he includes all human feelings and emotions which involve some bodily change, which he calls "corporeal transmutation."[40] In the will or rational appetite there may be a kind of joy which is not related to bodily delight, but this is not what Aquinas calls a passion in the strict sense, since it does not involve a bodily transmutation (*ST* I-II, q. 31, a. 4).

Like Aristotle, who says in Book 1 of the *Nicomachean Ethics* that the proper function of humanity is activity of the soul in accord with reason,[41] Aquinas considers conformity with reason to be the hallmark of virtuous activity.[42] Moral virtue is achieved when one's appetites conform to reason and when one has acquired a habit of acting in accord with reason, which means that one acts for ends which are goods specified by the natural law and uses appropriate means to attain those ends. A virtuous individual is one whose appetites and emotions have been trained over time to desire what is good according to the natural law and to avoid what is evil.

It may therefore be seen that Aquinas' virtue ethics requires that human reason have direct access to principles of the natural law without having to consult inclinations he attributes to the appetites, such as affective inclinations, desires, urges and dispositions of the will. If human reason were guided and directed by appetitive inclinations in gaining knowledge of the natural law, as claimed by the first group of interpreters mentioned earlier, then the very inclinations that reason is supposed to govern in the acquisition of moral virtue would themselves govern reason by informing it of the natural law. Thomas says that the first principles of the natural law, i.e. the naturally-known principles of practical reason, disclose to us the ends of the virtues.[43] Hence, if appetites directed reason to knowledge of the natural law, there would be a circularity in which reason, in order to be able to direct the appetites to virtuous ends, would itself have to seek direction from the appetites. If the notion of "conformity to reason" in Aquinas' virtue ethics is to be given meaningful content, reason cannot depend upon guidance from inclinations of the appetites for its knowledge of the natural law.

The theories of knowledge of a second group of interpreters, who seek to rationally derive precepts of the natural law from principles or propositions of theoretical or speculative reason, do not in principle clash with Aquinas' virtue ethics. Unlike the first group, most of them claim to get the content of the natural law *without* a circular appeal to inclinations of appetites which must be brought into conformity with reason's understanding of the natural law for there to be moral virtue. They do not, however, recognize the immediate intellectual intuition of self-evident precepts of the natural law according to the natural habit of *synderesis*, which makes the first principles known to all humans. Thus, they tend to have a hard time explaining how "plain persons" (to use a term coined by Alasdair MacIntyre) could ever acquire the virtues. These interpreters assert that Aquinas derives precepts of the natural law by discursive reasoning processes that tend to be difficult and convoluted, and which may even require knowledge of metaphysics, a science which relatively few people ever study.[44] Another problem for these interpreters is in explaining how the prescriptive "ought" principles of the natural law, i.e. first practical principles, could be logically derived from the descriptive "is" propositions of speculative reason. Aquinas' solution, which is to say that the first practical principles are "implanted in us by nature," and through the habit of *synderesis* are "naturally known without any investigation on the part of reason," i.e. that they are self-evident to the intellect without any discursive movement of reason, solves both problems.[45] It explains how plain persons naturally know the natural law and thus are equipped to acquire moral virtues, and it avoids the "is-ought" quandary.

Representatives of the third group of interpreters, in their "new natural law" theory, affirm that the virtues are essential to the moral life. In a 1987 essay by Germain Grisez, Joseph Boyle and John Finnis, the authors say that certain moral principles, called "modes of responsibility," "provide a standard by which one can evaluate character traits, to see which are genuine virtues."[46] In that essay, they do not claim to follow Aquinas in all respects.[47] For example, although they acknowledge the self-evidence of the natural law, they introduce moral principles that do not belong to the natural law and which cannot be deduced as conclusions from its self-evident precepts. Unlike Aquinas, they consider the natural law as pre-moral and as merely opening us to possibilities of a range of human goods to be pursued, without assigning any hierarchy of value. Their first moral principle is not taken from Aquinas, but rather stated in terms of acting for human goods in such a way as to choose and will "only those possibilities whose willing is compatible with a will toward integral human fulfillment.[48] Their "modes of responsibility" are its specifications. The virtues are "character traits" that conform to the modes of responsibility, but the authors do not follow Aquinas in saying that moral virtues are habits of the appetites in conformity with reason. In his recent article on Aquinas, Finnis acknowledges that moral virtues pertain to "one's whole will and character,"[49] but he has nothing to say about the passions or sensitive appetites as being perfected by moral virtue. While the virtue theory of this group of natural lawyers bears similarities to Aquinas' virtue ethics, their moral principles are of questionable origin, not self-evident principles of reason like the precepts of love and Aquinas' other natural law precepts. They have a relatively vague and unspecified notion of "character," in contrast to Aquinas' concrete references to both the will and the passions as the faculties perfected by moral virtue. Moreover, their notion of "integral human fulfillment," inasmuch as it does not recognize an ordered hierarchy of human goods, differs from Aquinas' emphasis on a single ultimate end or *telos* of humanity,[50] with the other goods ordered in relation to that ultimate end.[51]

In addition to the moral virtues, there is one intellectual virtue that is particularly important for human action: prudence. Prudence is a habit of the mind which enables the virtuous individual to make the right decisions in particular situations. It applies moral norms derived from the natural law and decides upon the means to attain the ends specified by the natural law. Aquinas considers prudence to be a moral virtue as well as an intellectual virtue because it moves the appetites with its commands. Aquinas considers it impossible to have moral virtue without prudence to direct the appetites, and impossible to have prudence without moral virtue to protect reason from being overrun by disordered passions. Hence the moral virtues and prudence go hand-in-hand.[52]

It is important to distinguish between prudence and synderesis. Synderesis is the *natural* habit of the intellect by which we know the first principles of the natural law, which specify the ends of human action. Prudence is an *acquired* habit of reason by which we apply the natural law in specific situations. We are born with synderesis, since it is a natural habit which is habitually present in us, but prudence can only be acquired with practice over time. Synderesis is said to appoint the ends of human action, which are the ends of the virtues, while prudence supplies us with the means to attain those ends.[53]

Thus far, we have considered the natural virtues, including moral virtues and intellectual virtues. In speaking of the natural virtues, Aquinas provides us with a more elaborate version of Aristotle's virtue ethics. However, Aquinas does not stop there. In Aquinas' ethical theory there are also supernatural virtues—faith, hope, and charity—which are neither inborn nor acquired over time by habituation. While the natural virtues are directed toward happiness in this life, the supernatural virtues are directed toward eternal salvation and union with God.

DEONTOLOGICAL, TELEOLOGICAL AND CONSEQUENTIALIST ASPECTS

We have seen that Aquinas' ethics is a virtue ethics that emphasizes the importance of character. We have also seen that it has the aspect of a deontological ethics which emphasizes compliance with rules or norms, since the principles of the natural law, known through the habit of synderesis, appoint the ends of the virtues and are the basic criteria for moral decision-making.

Aquinas' ethics may also be called teleological (directed toward a *telos* or end) because all human action is directed towards ends specified by the natural law. The first five questions of the I-II of the *Summa Theologiae* are concerned with man's last or ultimate end, which is said to be happiness. Following Aristotle, Aquinas says that the happiness that can be attained in this life through exercise of our natural powers "consists first and principally in contemplation, but secondarily in an operation of practical intellect directing human actions and passions, as stated in *Ethic.*, x. 7, 8" (*ST* I-II, q. 3, a. 5). In addition to the imperfect happiness attainable in this life, Aquinas also speaks of a perfect happiness that can only be attained in the life hereafter, which consists the vision of the divine essence (*ST* I-II, q. 3, a. 8). For now, however, let's look at what he says we can achieve in this life through our natural powers. It is important to notice that virtuous activity, i.e., the exercise of intellectual virtue in contemplation and of prudence in directing actions and passions according to the moral virtues, just *is* happiness. The end of human action cannot be separated from human action itself. Happiness in the Aristotelian sense, known as *eudainomia* in Greek, is often translated as "human flourishing." It is not merely a feeling of pleasure, although pleasure is associated with it. As Aristotle puts it in Book I of the *Nicomachean Ethics*, "happiness is some kind of activity of the soul in conformity with virtue."[54] The virtues are excellences, and the virtuous life is the most excellent life.

The main difference between Aquinas' ethics and the modern systems of Kant and Mill is that Aquinas, like Aristotle, does not separate virtuous action and happiness.[55] To state Kant's deontological ethics in an oversimplified but not entirely inaccurate form, the aim of moral action is to have a good will, which means acting in accord with the categorical imperative and doing our duty. According to Kant, the most praiseworthy actions involve denying our own happiness, at least in this life, for the sake of duty. To state Mill's utilitarian ethics as simply as possible, the aim of human action is happiness which is nothing more than a feeling of pleasure and absence of pain. A virtuous action is praiseworthy not for its own sake, but for its consequence, which is the maximization of pleasure. In each case, the virtuous activity is one thing and happiness is something else. Kant sacrifices happiness for the sake of right action. Mill sacrifices the idea of an action that is just or virtuous in itself for the sake of a consequence, namely the maximization of pleasure, whether it be for the individual, the society or the cosmos. While Kant's view seems overly severe in its attitude toward happiness, Mill's utilitarian ethics may be said to entail a certain loss of the sense of human dignity, since humans are reduced to vessels to be filled with pleasure. Missing in the utilitarian view is a recognition of the inherent dignity of the person to whom a just act is owed and who is likewise bound to act for the sake of justice itself, quite apart from any calculus of pleasure.[56]

Aquinas' ethical theory is not consequentialist in the sense of being solely directed toward consequences such as pleasure or other desirable outcomes. In Aquinas' ethics, the good or evil of an action depends primarily upon the object of the action (e.g. giving alms) and the will's intention of the end of the action (e.g. to help the poor, which is in accordance with the love of neighbour precept of the natural law) and secondarily on the circumstances.[57] If the object and the intention are both good, so is the action, even if the consequence is not good. Thus, if someone gives alms with a good intention, but the money is used by the recipient to purchase narcotics without knowledge or consent of the donor, the goodness of the donor's action is not affected.[58] But Aquinas does not entirely ignore the moral significance of consequences, as we read in the body of *ST* I-II, q. 20, a. 5. If consequences are foreseeable, or follow in the ordinary course of events from the very nature of the action, then they will increase either the goodness or the malice of the action.[59] Consequences are thus a factor in Aquinas' ethical theory, but not the sole and determining consideration.

CONCLUSION

In conclusion, it may be said that Aquinas provides us with a philosophical theory of human action that incorporates the best of deontological ethics, teleological or consequentialist ethics, and virtue ethics. In contrast, one might say that modern ethical theories tend to be relatively one-sided and fragmentary.

One further point ought to be made in conclusion. In addition to providing us with a philosophical ethics accessible to natural human reason, which may be implemented without the need to believe in a life hereafter, Aquinas provides us with a theological ethics based upon Christian revelation. We learn from Aquinas that the ultimate end of human life, perfect happiness in union with God, can only be attained in the life to come by the grace of God and through the infused supernatural virtues.

NOTES

1. *ST* I-II, q. 90, a. 1: "Law is a rule and measure of acts, whereby man is induced to act or is restrained from acting: for 'lex' (law) is derived from 'ligare' (to bind), because it binds one to act. Now the rule and measure of human acts is the reason, which is the first principle of human acts, as is evident from what has been stated above (q. 1, a. 1, ad 3); since it belongs to the reason to direct to the end, which is the first principle in all matters of action, according to the Philosopher (*Phys.* ii). Now that which is the principle in any genus, is the rule and measure of that genus: for instance, unity in the genus of numbers, and the first movement in the genus of movements. Consequently it follows that law is something pertaining to reason." Except where otherwise stated, all quotations from the *ST* are from the *Summa Theologica*, trans. Fathers of the English Dominican Province (New York: Benzinger Bros., 1948).

2. See *ST* I-II, q. 71, a. 2, including objections and replies. Parts of this article are quoted below.

3. *ST* I-II, q. 91, a. 2: "Wherefore, since all things subject to Divine providence are ruled and measured by the eternal law, as was stated above (a. 1); it is evident that all things partake somewhat of the eternal law, in so far as, namely, from its being imprinted on them, they derive their respective inclinations to their proper acts and ends. Now among all others, the rational creature is subject to Divine providence in the most excellent way, in so far as it partakes of a share of providence, by being provident both for itself and for others. Wherefore it has a share of the Eternal Reason, whereby it has a natural inclination to its proper act and end: and this participation of the eternal law in the rational creature is called the natural law. Hence the Psalmist after saying (Ps. 4:6): 'Offer up the sacrifice of justice,' as though someone asked what the works of justice are, adds: 'Many say, Who showeth us good things?' in answer to which question he says: 'The light of Thy countenance, O Lord, is signed upon us': thus implying that the light of natural reason, whereby we discern what is good and what is evil, which is the function of the natural law, is nothing else than an imprint on us of the Divine light. It is therefore evident that the natural law is nothing else than the rational creature's participation of the eternal law.'"

4. *ST* I-II, q. 91, a. 2, ad 3:"Even irrational animals partake in their own way of the Eternal Reason, just as the rational creature does. But because the rational creature partakes thereof in an intellectual and rational manner, therefore the participation of the eternal law in the rational creature is properly called a law, since a law is something pertaining to reason, as stated above (q. 90, a. 1). Irrational creatures, however, do not partake thereof in a rational manner, wherefore there is no participation of the eternal law in them, except by way of similitude." In "Le Droit naturel dans la pensée de Thomas d'Aquin," in *Droit naturel: relancer L'histoire*, ed. Xavier Dijon et al. (Brussels: Bruylant, 2008): 257-292, I examine Aquinas' use of the term *ius naturale*, which is sometimes used interchangeably with *lex naturalis*, but which in its more strict sense, in contrast to the *lex naturalis* proper to the rational creature, refers to the content of natural right that is common to all animals including humans, although unlike other animals humans apprehend it rationally not instinctually. In yet another sense, *ius naturale* refers to a state of nature prior to human art or ingenuity, such as the naked state of the human body prior to the invention of clothing (*ST* I-II, q. 94, a. 5, ad 3).

5. In this paragraph, I follow the summary of the main groups I provided in "Le Droit naturel dans la pensée de Thomas d'Aquin."

6. Most prominent among the first group is Jacques Maritain, who argues for a non-conceptual grasp of the natural law through connaturality or inclination in works such as *Man and the State* (Chicago: University of Chicago Press, 1951), "On Knowledge Through Connaturality," *The Review of Metaphysics* 4 (1951): 473-81 and *La Loi Naturelle ou Loi non Écrite*: texte inédit, établi par Georges Brazzola, (Fribourg: Éditions universitaires, 1986). Also worthy of mention is Rafael-Tomas Caldera, *Le jugement par inclination chez Saint Thomas d'Aquin* (Paris: J. Vrin, 1980).

7. This group includes Henry Veatch in *Swimming Against the Current of Contemporary Philosophy: Occasional Essays and Papers* (Washington, D.C.: The Catholic University of America Press, 1990) and Anthony J. Lisska in *Aquinas' Theory of Natural Law: An Analytic Reconstruction* (Oxford: Clarendon Press, 1996). Jan Aertsen suggests that the natural law becomes known to us through reflection on transcendental notions of being and the good in works such as "Natural Law in the Light of the Doctrine of the Transcendentals" in *Lex et Libertas: Freedom and Law According to St. Thomas Aquinas*, ed. L.J. Elders and K. Hedwig (Vatican City: Libreria editrice Vaticana, 1987), 99-112, and "Thomas Aquinas on the Good: The Relation between Metaphysics and Ethics," in *Aquinas' Moral Theory: Essays in Honor of Norman Kretzmann*, ed. Scott MacDonald and Eleonore Stump (Ithaca, NY: Cornell University Press, 1999), 235-53.

8. Representative works are Germain Grisez, "A Commentary on the Summa Theologiae, 1-2, Question 94, Article 2," *Natural Law Forum* 10 (1965): 168-201, and John Finnis, *Aquinas: Moral, Political and Legal Theory* (Oxford: Oxford University Press, 1998), especially at 79-94. My own view is that Grisez and Finnis correctly read Thomas in stating that the first principles are self-evident and known without inference through an insight of reason. I am thus closer to their position than to the positions of the other two main groups. I do not, however, agree with the emphasis that Grisez and Finnis give to experience of non-rational inclinations as a source of data for reason's insight, which seems to imply a derivation or disguised inference of precepts of law (although they deny it) from those inclinations. So far as they deny that the natural law is in any way innate in human reason, they leave us with these alternatives: it has its source in the pre-rational inclinations or is found nowhere in nature. Moreover, according to this third group, the first principles or precepts of the natural law are not moral principles because they are said to only specify human goods that are not moral goods (e.g., Grisez, 184). Thomas, on the other hand, treats all precepts of the natural law as moral precepts, human actions as synonymous with moral actions (*ST* I-II, q. 1, a. 3; q. 18, aa. 5 and 9) and the human good, founded in reason, as interchangeable with the moral good (*ST* I-II, q. 24, a. 3). Unlike Thomas, the members of this third group believe that they have to augment the precepts of the natural law with a further set of properly "moral" principles in order to ground their moral philosophy. See, for example, Germain Grisez, John Finnis and Joseph Boyle, "Practical Principles, Moral Truth, and Ultimate Ends," *The American Journal of Jurisprudence* 32 (1987): 123-25, 128-30. A somewhat revised formulation is provided by Finnis in the *Stanford Encyclopedia of Philosophy*, s.v. "Aquinas' Moral, Political and Legal Philosophy" (substantive revision Mon Sep 19, 2011), part 3.2, where Finnis accepts one of the precepts of love ("*love one's neighbour as oneself*") as Aquinas' "supreme moral principle."

9. In regard to principles of the natural law being implanted by God or nature in human reason where they pre-exist or are said to be innate, see, for example, *Scriptum super libros Sententiarum*, III, d. 33, q. 2, a. 4, qc. 4; d. 37, q. 1, a. 1, ad 3; d. 37, q. 1, a. 3; *Scriptum super libros Sententiarum*, IV, d. 33, q. 1, a. 1; *Quaestiones disputatae de veritate* (*De veritate*), q. 10, a. 6, ad 6; q. 11, a. 1; q. 11, a. 3; q. 16, a. 1; *Summa contra gentiles* (*SCG*) III, 46, n. 4; *ST* I, q. 79, a. 12; *ST* I-II, q. 90, a. 4, ad 1; q. 93, a. 2, s.c.; q. 100, a. 3; *ST* II-II, q. 47, a. 6.

10. For example, J. Durantel's discussion of Aquinas' theory of knowledge in *Le Retour à Dieu* (Paris: Librairie Félix Alcan, 1918), 156-69, treats the first principles as innate in human intelligence. Denis J.M Bradley speaks of the natural law as "innate first principles of practical reason" and of "'innate' principles of *synderesis*" in *Aquinas on the Twofold Human Good: Reason and Human Happiness in Aquinas' Moral Science* (Washington, D.C.: The Catholic University of America Press, 1997), at 134 and 292. I have argued in my doctoral dissertation ("Thomas Aquinas and Knowledge of the First Principles of the Natural Law," The Catholic University of America, 2007) for a literal reading of those texts which say that the first principles are innate or divinely implanted in human reason. Nevertheless, the innate first principles are not said to be known in the sense of being actually considered except on occasion of reception of a sensory image (*phantasma*), and thus Thomas says that "cognitio principiorum provenit nobis ex sensu" (*ST* I-II, q. 51, a. 1).

11. In so doing, I summarize points made in my doctoral dissertation referenced in the previous note.

12. *ST* I-II, q. 94, a. 2: "As stated above (q. 91, a. 3), the precepts of the natural law are to the practical reason, what the first principles of demonstrations are to the speculative reason; because both are self-evident principles."

13. *ST* I-II, q. 90, a. 4, ad 1: "The natural law is promulgated by the very fact that God instilled it into man's mind so as to be known by him naturally." See also *ST* I, q. 79, a. 12; *ST* I-II, q. 91, a. 3, ad 2 and q. 94, a. 2

14. *ST* I-II, q. 94, a. 1, ad 3: "[S]ometimes a man is unable to make use of that which is in him habitually, on account of some impediment: thus, on account of sleep, a man is unable to use the habit of science. In like manner, through the deficiency of his age, a child cannot use the habit of understanding of principles, or the natural law, which is in him habitually." See also the *sed contra* to q. 94, a. 1, where it is stated that "the natural law is in infants and in the damned who cannot act by it." Aquinas distinguishes among things that are potentially, habitually and actually present in our minds in *ST* I, q. 79, a. 6, ad 3. If it is not present in our minds at all, but might be, it is *potentially* in our minds. If we are aware of it, and considering it, it is *actually* present. If it is retained in the mind, but we are not aware of it right now (like a memory before we recall it), it is *habitually* present.

15. See *ST* I, q. 79, a. 12 and *ST* I-II, q. 94, a. 1.

16. Although the first principles are said to be innate and implanted in our minds by God or nature, they cannot be actually known unless we first receive something from the senses. Thus, the habits of understanding first principles (including the habit of synderesis in the case of the natural law) only operate in the context of sense experience, and need to be triggered by a relevant experience. See, for example, *ST* I-II, q. 51, a. 1 and *De veritate* (*Quaestiones disputatae de veritate*) q. 11, a. 1 and q. 16, a. 1. For an English translation of *De veritate*, see *Truth*, trans. Robert W. Mulligan, James V. McGlynn, Robert W. Schmidt (Chicago, Regnery, 1952-54; reprint: Indianapolis: Hackett, 1994), especially vol. 2 (qq. 10-20).

17. In a number of texts (e.g., *De veritate* q. 15, a. 1 and q. 16, a.1; *ST* I, q. 79, aa. 8 and 12, also discussed below in note 21) Aquinas distinguishes the act of understanding (*intellectus*) from discursive reasoning (*ratio*), and explains that there are two distinct movements of discursive reason. The first movement is called *inventio* or discovery, which *begins* from an understanding of first principles and moves to conclusions. The second is a movement back from conclusions to principles by analysis (*resolutio*) in order to attain certain judgment. In the movement of analysis, which *concludes* with an act of understanding, the process of reasoning and the principles are made explicit. Aquinas says in *De veritate*, q. 11, a. 1 that belief or opinion which falls short of certain knowledge (*scientia*) is in some way caused by self-evident first principles, but he adds that such belief or opinion may follow from an argument proposed by another that "does not make it clear that [first principles] are included (*includi non manifestantur*)." In such a case, prior to analysis back to first principles, knowledge of them may be said to be implicit.

18. *ST* I-II, q. 94, a. 2: "Hence this is the first precept of law, that 'good is to be done and pursued, and evil is to be avoided.' All other precepts of the natural law are based upon this: so that whatever the practical reason naturally apprehends as man's good (or evil) belongs to the precepts of the natural law as something to be done or avoided."

19. Ibid., ad 2: "All the inclinations of any parts whatsoever of human nature, e.g. of the concupiscible and irascible parts, in so far as they are ruled by reason, belong to the natural law, and are reduced to one first precept, as stated above: so that the precepts of the natural law are many in themselves, but are based on one common foundation."

20. When Thomas speaks of the self-evident precepts of the natural law at the beginning of *ST* I-II, q. 94, a. 2, he speaks of them in the plural.

21. *ST* I, q. 79, aa. 8 and 12, for a discussion of how we know first principles in a simple act of apprehension, also called understanding. This same topic is taken up in more detail by Aquinas in *De veritate*, particularly in q. 15, a. 1 and q. 16, a. 1 and in texts cited in the next two footnotes. The Latin term *intellectus*, which means understanding or intellect, is sometimes contrasted to *ratio* which means reason, especially in the sense of discursive reason. While the act of understanding or *intellectus* is a simple act of apprehension or insight, discursive reason moves from one thing to another, e.g. from premises to conclusions. On the other hand, the acts of *intellectus* and *ratio* belong to the same power, usually called *ratio* (reason) but also called *intellectus* (intellect).

22. *De veritate*, q. 10, a. 8: "We see (*intuemur*) this inviolable truth in its likeness which is impressed on our mind to the extent that we know some things as self-evident. We examine all other things with reference to these, judging of them according to these." *De veriate*, q. 11, a. 1, ad 12: "[T]he mind sees certain things immediately, those which are self-evident (*sed quaedam statim videt quae sunt per se nota*), in which are contained certain other things which it can understand only by using reason to unfold those things which are implicitly contained in principles."

23. In *De veritate*, q. 8, a. 15, Aquinas says that "we know principles by simple intuition without discourse."

24. See Aristotle, *Posterior Analytics*, Book I, chs. 2-3. If there are no self-evident first principles, which Aristotle calls primary and indemonstrable premises, then we can have no real proof of anything. If even the first principles

had to be proved by demonstration, we would have only an infinite regress of arguments, or a circle.

25. *ST* I, q. 79, a. 12. In the translation of the English Dominican Fathers, the principles are said to be "bestowed on us by nature." However, Latin word used by Aquinas, *indita*, is more literally translated as "implanted" rather than as "bestowed."

26. See *ST* I-II, q. 100, a. 3, obj. 1 and ad 1; q. 100, a. 5, ad 1.

27. *ST* I, q. 2, a. 1, ad 1: "To know that God exists in a general and confused way is implanted in us by nature, inasmuch as God is man's beatitude. For man naturally desires happiness, and what is naturally desired by man must be naturally known to him. This, however, is not to know absolutely that God exists; just as to know that someone is approaching is not the same as to know that Peter is approaching, even though it is Peter who is approaching; for many there are who imagine that man's perfect good which is happiness, consists in riches, and others in pleasures, and others in something else."

28. *ST* I-II, q. 27, a. 2, s.c.: "Augustine proves (De Trin. x, 1,2) that 'none can love what he does not know.'" See also the body of the same article: "As stated above (a. 1), good is the cause of love, as being its object. But good is not the object of the appetite, except as apprehended. And therefore love demands some apprehension of the good that is loved. For this reason the Philosopher (*Ethic.* ix, 5,12) says that bodily sight is the beginning of sensitive love: and in like manner the contemplation of spiritual beauty or goodness is the beginning of spiritual love. Accordingly knowledge is the cause of love for the same reason as good is, which can be loved only if known."

29. *Contemporary Moral Problems*, 10th ed. (Boston: Wadsworth Cengage Learning, 2012), 4.

30. The distinction between what is "from nature" (*a natura*) and what is "in accord with nature" (*secundum naturum*) is made by Aquinas in *ST* I-II q. 71, a. 2, ad 2.

31. *ST* I-II, q. 62, a. 3: "As stated above (a. 1), the theological virtues direct man to supernatural happiness in the same way as by the natural inclination man is directed to his connatural end. Now the latter happens in respect of two things. First, in respect of the reason or intellect, in so far as it contains the first universal principles which are known to us by the natural light of the intellect, and which are reason's starting-point, both in speculative and in practical matters. Secondly, through the rectitude of the will which tends naturally to good as defined by reason." The first principles in practical matters are, of course, the first precepts or principles of the natural law (*ST* I-II, q. 94, a. 2).

32. *ST* I-II, q. 95, a. 2: "But it must be noted that something may be derived from the natural law in two ways: first, as a conclusion from premises, secondly, by way of determination of certain generalities. The first way is like to that by which, in sciences, demonstrated conclusions are drawn from the principles: while the second mode is likened to that whereby, in the arts, general forms are particularized as to details: thus the craftsman needs to determine the general form of a house to some particular shape. Some things are therefore derived from the general principles of the natural law, by way of conclusions; e.g., that 'one must not kill' may be derived as a conclusion from the principle that 'one should do harm to no man': while some are derived therefrom by way of determination; e.g. the law of nature has it that the evil-doer should be punished; but that he be punished in this or that way, is a determination of the law of nature.

Accordingly both modes of derivation are found in the human law. But those things which are derived in the first way, are contained in human law not as emanating therefrom exclusively, but have some force from the natural law also. But those things which are derived in the second way, have no other force than that of human law."

33. *ST* II-II, q. 66, a. 7: "Nevertheless, if the need be so manifest and urgent, that it is evident that the present need must be remedied by whatever means be at hand (for instance when a person is in some imminent danger, and there is no other possible remedy), then it is lawful for a man to succor his own need by means of another's property, by taking it either openly or secretly: nor is this properly speaking theft or robbery."

34. *ST* I-II, q. 94, a. 4: "As stated above (aa. 2, 3), to the natural law belongs those things to which a man is inclined naturally: and among these it is proper to man to be inclined to act according to reason. Now the process of reason is from the common to the proper, as stated in *Phys.* i. The speculative reason, however, is differently situated in this matter, from the practical reason. For, since the speculative reason is busied chiefly with the necessary things, which cannot be otherwise than they are, its proper conclusions, like the universal principles, contain the truth without fail. The practical reason, on the other hand, is busied with contingent matters, about which human actions are concerned: and consequently, although there is necessity in the general principles, the more we descend to matters of detail, the more frequently we encounter defects. Accordingly then in speculative matters truth is the same in all men, both as to principles and as to conclusions: although the truth is not known to all as regards the conclusions, but only as regards the principles which are called common notions. But in matters of action, truth or practical rectitude is not the same for all, as to matters of detail, but only as to the general principles: and where there is the same rectitude in matters of detail, it is not equally known to all.

It is therefore evident that, as regards the general principles whether of speculative or of practical reason, truth or rectitude is the same for all, and is equally known by all. As to the proper conclusions of the speculative reason, the truth is the same for all, but is not equally known to all: thus it is true for all that the three angles of a triangle are together equal to two right angles, although it is not known to all. But as to the proper conclusions of the practical reason, neither is the truth or rectitude the same for all, nor, where it is the same, is it equally known by all. Thus it is right and true for all to act according to reason: and from this principle it follows as a proper conclusion, that goods entrusted to another should be restored to their owner. Now this is true for the majority of cases: but it may happen in a particular case that it would be injurious, and therefore unreasonable, to restore goods held in trust; for instance, if they are claimed for the purpose of fighting against one's country. And this principle will be found to fail the more, according as we descend further into detail, e.g. if one were to say that goods held in trust should be restored with such and such a guarantee, or in such and such a way; because the greater the number of conditions added, the greater the number of ways in which the principle may fail, so that it be not right to restore or not to restore.

Consequently we must say that the natural law, as to general principles, is the same for all, both as to rectitude and as to knowledge. But as to certain matters of detail, which are conclusions, as it were, of those general principles, it is the same for all in the majority of cases, both as to rectitude and as to knowledge; and yet in some few cases it may fail, both as to rectitude, by reason of certain obstacles (just as natures subject to generation and corruption fail in some few cases on account of some obstacle), and as to knowledge, since:

> in some the reason is perverted by passion, or evil habit, or an evil disposition of nature; thus formerly, theft, although it is expressly contrary to the natural law, was not considered wrong among the Germans, as Julius Caesar relates (*De Bello Gall.* vi).

35. The prohibition of theft, like other precepts of the Decalogue, is not considered by Aquinas to be one of the self-evident first general principles, but is said to be known immediately after slight reflection (*ST* I-II, q. 100, a. 3). The same point is illustrated q. 95, a. 2 in the case of the prohibition against murder, "which may be derived as a conclusion from the principle that *one should do harm to no man*."

36. See Gregory Doolan, "The First Principles of the Natural Law," in *Reassessing the Liberal State: Reading Maritain's "Man and the State,"* ed. Timothy Fuller and John T. Hittinger (Washington, D.C.: The Catholic University of America Press, 2001), 136. Doolan contends that in the case of the Germans discussed in q. 94, a. 4 who did not consider theft a crime, that Aquinas does not mean to say that they were ignorant of the precept, *Thou shalt not steal*, but rather that they were ignorant of its application in the case of stealing from other tribes or peoples. "Such ignorance, therefore," Doolan says, "is an error concerning the minor premise of a practical syllogism – in short, it is a deductive error."

37. Deontic theories may be understood to include both deontological and consequentialist theories.

38. See Louis Pojman, *Ethics: Discovering Right and Wrong*, 5th ed. (Belmont, CA: Thomson Wadsworth, 2006), chapter 8. Pojman speaks at p. 165 of "pure aretaic ethics" in which he says that, "Moral principles or duties are derived from the virtues." In contrast is what Pojman calls the "standard deontic view" in which action-guiding principles are primary and virtues are merely derivative. Thirdly, he speaks of a "complementary ethics" which recognizes that both virtues and principles have intrinsic value. Aquinas' view is close to the third view in recognizing that virtuous character is a good in its own right, and that it is not enough for one's external actions to be according to principles.

39. See *ST* I, q. 79, a 12; *ST* I-II, q. 51, a. 1; q. 63, a. 1; q. 63, a. 2, ad 3.

40. See *ST* I-II, q. 22, a. 3: "As stated above (a. 1) passion is properly to be found where there is corporeal transmutation. This corporeal transmutation is found in the act of the sensitive appetite, and is not only spiritual, as in the sensitive apprehension, but also natural." In q. 23, a. 4, Aquinas speaks of eleven passions of the soul, including the concupiscible passions of love and hatred, desire and aversion, joy and sadness and the irascible passions of hope and despair, fear and daring, and anger.

41. 1098a5-10.

42. *ST* I-II, q. 58, a. 2: "Hence just as the appetite is the principle of human acts, in so far as it partakes of reason, so are moral habits to be considered virtues in so far as they are in conformity with reason." Also, q. 58, a. 4: "Moral virtue perfects the appetitive part of the soul by directing it to good as defined by reason."

43. *ST* II-II, q. 47, a. 6: "in the practical reason, certain things pre-exist, as naturally-known principles, and such are the ends of the moral virtues."

44. See *The Division and Methods of the Sciences*, ed. and trans. by Armand Maurer, 4th ed. (Toronto: Pontifical Institute of Medieval Studies, 1986), Appendix 2, pp. 95-102. The editor has collected texts of Aquinas on the order of learning of the sciences. Metaphysics, also called divine science, comes last in the order of learning, *after* the study of moral science or ethics, due to its abstract and difficult topics concerning matters which "go beyond the imagination and require a vigorous mind" (102).

45. Quotations in this sentence are from *ST* I-II, q. 79, a. 12, where Aquinas discusses the operation of the natural habit of *synderesis*, whereby the first practical principles become actually known to the intellect. In place of the English Dominican translation of *nobise esse indita* ("bestowed on us by nature"), I have substituted the more literal "implanted in us by nature."

46. "Practical Principles, Moral truth, and Ultimate Ends," *The American Journal of Jurisprudence* 32 (1987): 129.

47. Ibid., 99.

48. Ibid., 128. Cf. note 9, *supra*. Finnis more recently (2011) says that the precept of love of neighbor is Aquinas' "supreme moral principle."

49. "Aquinas' Moral, Political and Legal Philosophy," section 4.1.

50. See my discussion of Aquinas' teleology below under the heading "Deontological, Teleological and Consequentialist Aspects."

51. *ST* I-II, q. 13, a. 3, ad 2: "There is but one last end (*ultimus finis*). Accordingly wherever there are several ends, they can be the subject of choice, in so far as they are ordained to a further end (*ulteriorem finem*)." As compared to the translation of the English Dominicans, John A. Oesterle more precisely renders *ultimus finis* and *ulteriorem finem* as "ultimate end" in his translation of the "Treatise on Happiness" of Saint Thomas Aquinas (Notre Dame: University of Notre Dame Press, 1983).

52. See *ST* I-II, q. 58, aa. 4-5. For a more detailed account of the operation of prudence and its relationship to the moral virtues, with references to the texts of Aquinas, see David J. Klassen, "Application of the Natural Law in the Thought of St. Thomas Aquinas," *Études maritainiennes – Maritain Studies* 24 (2008): 19–34, especially at 29–32.

53. See *ST* II-II, q. 47, a. 6, "Whether prudence appoints the end to the moral virtues?" including objections and replies for Aquinas' most complete discussion of the different roles of synderesis and prudence.

54. 1099b25-30.

55. This has been pointed out by Robert Sokolowski, "Virtue and Human Action," (course lectures, The Catholic University of America, Washington, D.C., Spring Term, 2002).

56. A contemporary American philosopher influenced by Kant, John Rawls (1921-2002), put it this way: "Each person possesses an inviolability founded on justice that even the welfare of society as a whole cannot override . . . .The rights secured by justice are not subject to political bargaining or to the calculus of social interests," *A Theory of Justice* (Harvard University Press, 1971), 3, as quoted by Pojman, 150.

57. See *ST* I-II, qq. 18–21 for Aquinas' analysis of good and evil in human actions.

58. *ST* I-II, q. 20, a. 5, s.c.: "The consequences do not make an action that was evil, to be good; nor one that was good, to be evil. For instance, if a man give an alms to a poor man who makes bad use of the alms by committing a sin,

this does not undo the good done by the giver; and, in like manner, if a man bear patiently a wrong done to him, the wrongdoer is not thereby excused."

59.   *ST* I-II, q. 20, a. 5: "The consequences of an action are either foreseen or not. If they are foreseen, it is evident that they increase the goodness or malice. For when a man foresees that many evils may follow from his action, and yet does not therefore desist therefrom, this shows his will to be all the more inordinate.

But if the consequences are not foreseen, we must make a distinction. Because if they follow from the nature of the action and in the majority of cases, in this respect, the consequences increase the goodness or malice of that action: for it is evident that an action is specifically better, if better results can follow from it; and specifically worse, if it is of a nature to produce worse results. On the other hand, if the consequences follow by accident and seldom, then they do not increase the goodness or malice of the action: because we do not judge of a thing according to that which belongs to it by accident, but only according to that which belongs to it of itself."

THE NATURAL LAW: THEORETICAL INSIGHTS AND PROSPECTS FOR RENEWAL FROM G.E.M. ANSCOMBE

Zachary Mabee

INTRODUCTION

I aim in this article is to present a summary of G.E.M. Anscombe's work on the 'natural law' (hereafter NL) in particular and the broader "law conception of ethics" (hereafter LCE). In doing so, I aspire to argue for both the distinctive theoretical contributions of this work and its relevance for resuscitating and developing the tradition of natural law inquiry in the current-day academic, philosophical milieu. There are various challenges that await this study. Perhaps a first and most basic one is where and how to begin and, relatedly, with what sort of scope to conduct it. For Anscombe did not write at length or systematically about NL/LCE. In fact, she wrote only one brief four-page essay whose title contains 'natural law,' though several of her essays—particularly those relating to sexual and military ethics — treat it significantly.[1] In attempting to summarize and draw together some of her scattered musings on the topic, then, I will proceed modestly, looking first and chiefly at those texts in which she explicitly discusses NL/LCE. I will then move, as is appropriate, to related topics, such as issues of normativity and virtue in ethics. My aim throughout will be, again, to appraise her thought on the topic both for its distinctive theoretical contributions and also for its potential to revitalize a tradition of inquiry, particularly within the contemporary academic, philosophical climate.

WHAT IS THE 'NATURAL LAW'?

Anscombe treats of the NL as such in several essays, though the discussions are often in passing rather than serving as the focus of her argument. Consider, to begin, this passage from her essay "The Justice of the Present War Examined":

> The idea of natural moral law is one which modern men have lost; but without it they cannot live in peace within themselves, or socially or internationally. For the natural law is the law of man's own nature, showing how he must choose to act in matters where his will is free, if his nature is to be properly fulfilled. It is the proper use of his functions; their misuse or perversion is sin. . . .
>
> To those who believe in God it will rightly appear that His law, the eternal law, has its reflection in the ordered activity of Creation, that 'law of nature' which is the truth of things. In man, this activity is not wholly determined, but there is an element of choice. Thus far, "to him the law is proposed; it is not imposed upon him." But it is not less law for that; it binds because it is the law of his nature. And in what it consists he can discover by reason, checked and guaranteed by the divine revelation of Scripture. Aquinas called it "the participation in the eternal law of the rational creature" . . . .the law in him from his creation . . . .if man does not live according to his proper nature he will not attain his proper end.[2]

In a similar vein, consider this passage from her noteworthy, controversial piece "Contraception and Chastity":

> 'Natural law' is simply a way of speaking about the whole of morality, used by Catholic thinkers because they believe the general precepts of morality are *laws* promulgated by God our Creator in the enlightened human understanding when it is thinking in general terms about what are good and what are bad actions. That is to say, the discoveries of reflection and reasoning when we think straight about these things *are* God's legislation to us (whether we realize this or not).
>
> In thinking about conduct we have to advert to laws of nature in another sense. That is, to very general and

very well-known facts of nature, and also to ascertained scientific laws. For example, the resources of earth have to be worked on to supply our needs and enhance our lives: this is a general and well-known fact of nature. Hence there needs to be control over resources by definite owners . . . and this is the institution of property. . . . The institution of property has as its corollary the 'law of nature' in the ethical sense, the sense of a law of morality, which forbids stealing. It's useful, very useful, to get clear about all this.[3]

Consider one final representative passage, this one from her essay "Contraception and Natural Law":

[T]he notion 'against the natural law' is simply equivalent in extension to the notion 'what is wrong.' Belief in the natural law is the belief that the discoveries of reason about ethics are the promulgation of laws to the rational creature by the Creator. The content of the natural law is thus simply the content of ethics, so far as this is independent of revelation. . . . .It is wrong, or, in the law conception of ethics, against the natural law, if an adult of sound mind leads an unexamined life . . . .There is a range of sexual sins called 'sins against nature.' The concept of natural law is not especially closely involved in the notion of that type of sin. Those sins are not called 'sins against nature' *because* they are 'violations of natural law': *any* sin is that.[4]

We do well to pause here and take stock of these passages, which are some of Anscombe's clearest and most content-rich about NL (and LCE) as such. We might first note, as something of a background point, that Anscombe seems to see herself as expounding a basically traditional Catholic, Thomistic take on NL, though she views its broader contemporary presentation — for instance in "thoughtless Catholic apologetic of recent times"[5] — as sometimes wanting. She seems to see herself, that is, as expounding a great tradition of NL thought, but as doing so in a renewed, perhaps more refined sort of way. Second, we note that she sees adherence to NL as basic to human nature and flourishing, such that, if one fails to adhere to it, he will lack internal "peace" as well as harmony with other people. Indeed, NL is the law of "man's own nature," which establishes certain boundaries on the exercise of his freedom, so that he engages it to the fulfillment, rather than to the detriment, of his nature. It is the law or "truth" of the nature of beings of his kind, who have particular faculties, powers, potentialities, and the like.[6] Third, Anscombe seems quite adamant that the NL is indeed properly (though perhaps not always directly in practice) grasped and adhered to as law, which we participate in by our rational faculties.[7] (Ultimately, as the texts make clear, she thinks it to be our rational participation in the eternal law of God, our creator.) It thus presents itself to us, so to speak, as binding and carrying a certain normative force, though we also engage in free decisions to follow it (or not). Finally, we note that, in concert with the basic character of NL, Anscombe seems to want to identify NL with the whole of ethics or morality, such that *any* sin, wrongdoing, or moral offense meaningfully counts as a sin "against nature."[8] NL therefore seems to have a comprehensive scope, such that we can speak of it as coextensive with ethics in general, as she notes.

Any number of comments or threads of discussion could easily develop from this initial summary of Anscombe's views on NL. I want to develop one in particular, however, in accord with the aims I stated at the outset of this essay. For I noted that I would like to take stock of Anscombe's views on the NL and the LCE, but to do so with a mind to seeing how her views might help to advance philosophical discussions on the matter within the current academic milieu. In the foregoing passages and summary points that we extracted from them, we see a curious trend, given their piecemeal, scattershot treatment in Anscombe's works. (For as I noted, she treated them only within other more precise pieces on sexuality, war, or trends within academic philosophy.) Indeed, it seems as though, in these passages, Anscombe is quite clearly and strongly identifying NL (or LCE) with the whole of ethics, such that, at least at a basic theoretical level, one need not offer any sort of superior or rival account to NL (and LCE); that it is, of its own accord — at least if expounded and defended well — quite sufficient for ethical theorizing and deliberation. If this is the case, though, we might immediately ask why a noteworthy percentage of ordinary people and probably nearly all academic philosophers (at least of the last few generations) fail to see NL (or LCE) as credible. Anscombe attempts to address this concern and particularly to answer some of the complaints and objections of academic philosophers, at least in her landmark essay "Modern Moral Philosophy," which I think also offers us a hermeneutical key for her take on NL and LCE.

LAW, ETHICS, AND "MODERN MORAL PHILOSOPHY"

We have noted a curious situation in the foregoing texts of Anscombe: her apparent insistence on NL as coextensive with the whole of ethics and yet her also apparently tangential mentions of it. In "Modern Moral Philosophy," however, (hereafter "MMP"), she provides what I take to be a hermeneutical key for her preferred approach to reintegrating NL into philosophical discussions of morality (and so, presumably, academic and everyday discourse). She begins "MMP" by clarifying her chief aims in the essay:

> I will begin by stating three theses which I present in this paper. The first is that it is not profitable at present to do moral philosophy; that should be laid aside at any rate until we have an adequate philosophy of psychology, in which we are conspicuously lacking. The second is that the concepts of obligation — *moral* obligation and *moral* duty, that is to say — and of what is *morally* right and wrong, and of the *moral* sense of 'ought,' ought to be jettisoned if this is psychologically possible; because they are survivals from an earlier conception of ethics which no longer generally survives, and are only harmful without it.[9]

"MMP" seems to be, in many philosophers' minds, one of Anscombe's most searing, resounding essays, as well as something of a paradigm-shifting piece in the field of moral philosophy or ethical theory.[10] She commences it by claiming, as we have just seen, that she is thoroughly dissatisfied with the present philosophical psychology or anthropology that undergirds various ethical theories. She treats this topic at greater length in various other essays and books.[11] More for our purposes here, her second point of critique about obligation is particularly relevant. Anscombe clarifies, a bit later in the essay, that such concepts with their specifically moral connotations are more or less vestiges of a Jewish-Christian (or even classical-Stoic) law conception of ethics, which she characterizes thus:

> To have a *law* conception of ethics is to hold that what is needed for conformity with the virtues — failure in which is the mark of being bad *qua* man (and not merely, say *qua* craftsman of logician) — that what is needed for *this*, is required by divine law. Naturally it is not possible to have such a conception unless you believe in God as a law-giver; like Jews, Stoics and Christians. But if such a conception is dominant for many centuries, and then is given up, it is a natural result that the concepts of 'obligation' being bound or required as by a law, should remain though they had lost their root; and if the word 'ought' has become invested in certain concepts with the sense of 'obligation,' it too will remain to be spoken with a special emphasis and a special feeling in these contexts.[12]

Though she devotes much of "MMP" to criticizing the work of Hume and various other modern ethicists, Anscombe is quite insistent that he and various other thinkers of a similar mind did a philosophical service in critiquing the going notions of the moral 'ought' and moral law that they encountered in their day:

> Hume discovered the situation in which the notion of 'obligation' survived, and the word 'ought' was invested with that peculiar force having which it is said to be used

> in a 'moral' sense, but in which the belief in divine law had long since been abandoned: for it was substantially given up among Protestants at the time of the Reformation. The situation, if I am right, was the interesting one of the survival of a concept outside the framework...that made it a really intelligible one. . . .
>
> I should judge that Hume and our present-day ethicists had done a considerable service by showing that no content could be found in the notion of 'morally ought'; if it were not that the latter philosophers try to find an alternative (very fishy) content and to retain the psychological force of the term. It would be most reasonable to drop it. It has no reasonable sense outside a law conception of ethics; they are not going to maintain such a conception; and you can do ethics without it, as is shown by the example of Aristotle. It would be a great improvement if, instead of 'morally wrong,' one always named a genus such as 'untruthful,' 'unchaste' 'unjust.' We should no longer ask whether doing something was 'wrong,' passing directly from some description of an action to this notion; we should ask whether, e.g., it was unjust; and the answer would sometimes be clear at once.[13]

In a word, Anscombe is quite convinced that LCE is properly intelligible within a broader tradition or context in which God is held (among other things) to be the ethical legislator. Since the Judeo-Christian context for LCE was lost in the West (by, say, the time of the Reformation), philosophers have variously — but in futility, she thinks — attempted to offer ingenious quasi-legalistic interpretations of morality. (Kant, for instance, proffers what Anscombe takes to be the rather bizarre and inept notion of self-legislation in morality.)[14] We find such an approach, according to Anscombe, in G.E. Moore and his followers, who attempt to ascribe moral rectitude to the realization of those states of affairs that a consequentialist calculus yields.[15]

If we take this general critique of Anscombe's — drawn here from "MMP" — at its word, we can gather several theoretical insights into the ethical enterprise as well as, in accordance with my aim in this paper, some practical insight about how to revitalize NL or LCE. First, it seems quite clear from these passages that a robust LCE, for Anscombe, is only practicable and intelligible with a certain underlying cultural-religious context or backdrop — which historically in the West was attributable to the Jewish and Christian religions, or in the ancient world linked to the Stoics, among others. The key feature, at any rate, of such a cultural-religious context or backdrop is its pervasive or fundamental appreciation of God as legislator or law-giver, as the one who promulgates relevant (natural and divine) laws. As she notes quite pithily later in "MMP," "You cannot be under a law unless it has been promulgated to you; and the thinkers who believe in 'natural divine law' held that it was promulgated to every grown man in his knowledge of good and evil."[16]

So this initial key theoretical insight from Anscombe is really a contextual one: that NL or LCE depends upon a cultural-religious backdrop in which a divine legislator is acknowledged and whose role is taken seriously in practical and theoretical deliberations. Without such a context, she seems willing to concede that "it would be most reasonable to drop it [i.e., NL/LCE]."[17] Duncan Richter captures this insight quite nicely:

> What Anscombe objects to is a secular use of religious *concepts* (not mere words). There is a religious tradition according to which certain kinds of action are commanded and others are forbidden by God. Within this tradition, the human race has an historical relationship with God, in which various promises have been made, covenants agreed to, and so on. It makes sense, therefore, to talk within this tradition of being bound or obliged to do this or that. It makes no sense, however, to think that one is equally bound in just the same way if this tradition is rejected or bracketed, set aside, for philosophical purposes. It

is at best misleading, therefore, if anyone means to do philosophy in a religiously non-committal way but still asks what acts are forbidden, sinful, permissible, and so on. One problem with such language is that it seems to imply the very religious framework that is explicitly disavowed by the philosophers in question who use it.[18]

This cautionary point seems to be quite relevant for those attempting to work within and NL/LCE tradition. I take it that Anscombe would not object to work on topics within this tradition as such among, say, groups of Catholic (or otherwise Christian or Jewish, or even neo-Stoic) thinkers who share and practice — as much as one can in the contemporary world — this germane context or background.[19] It does seem, however, that she thinks it appropriate — given the cultural-religious circumstances of our day — to proceed with ethical deliberation in broader, less religious contexts (i.e., in various academic and other popular contexts that do not accept the existence of God and his role as legislator) with a method that broadly comes from Aristotle and his virtue-based tradition of ethical inquiry.

Before turning to this tradition, however, and Anscombe's refined retrieval of it, I should note another theoretical point of importance from this current thread. We note here in "MMP," as we also did in some of her other texts,[20] that Anscombe stresses a rather traditional distinction in her discussion of NL: that NL is really eternal, divine law (or, at any rate, humanly relevant parts or precepts of it) insofar as or presented as apprehensible by ("enlightened") human reason. As we saw with the preceding contextual point, Anscombe seems quite adamant here that an account of NL/LCE that lacks this connection to divine authority is ultimately a weak or deficient account of it as law. She is rather insistent, in other words, that a philosophical account of natural or divine law must include a relevant account of this law's legislator and various connections between him and his injunctions.[21]

VIRTUE AND LAW?

We have therefore as a first key insight from "MMP" that Anscombe no longer thinks NL/LCE to be a generally sustainable ethical program — at least within broader, not-exclusively-religious discourse contexts — principally given endemic and thoroughgoing confusion and lack of precision regarding the notion of law and how it relates to morality. She does expressly, however, prefer another approach to ethics, specifically that of Aristotle, which depends crucially and in the first instance on virtue- (or vice-) oriented descriptions of actions. According to this approach to ethics, we evaluate various actions according to their positively embodying some or other virtue, or their failure to do so. An instance of lying, e.g., would be cast not simply or mainly as wrong or illicit, but instead as dishonest, untruthful, or unjust. So she says, as we have already seen,

> It would be a great improvement if, instead of "morally wrong," one always named a genus such as "untruthful," "unchaste," "unjust." We should no longer ask whether doing something was "wrong," passing directly from some description of an action to this notion; we should ask whether, e.g., it was unjust; and the answer would sometimes be clear at once.[22]

In a key way, Anscombe sees virtue-based descriptions of actions as richer than their legal counterparts. To say that one's telling a lie is wrong or illicit tells us (particularly in the latter's case) that it violates a norm and legal precept against lying, but it does not tell us much more. To say, however, that such an action is untruthful or unjust to one's interlocutor offers a more descriptively rich account with which, from a philosophical perspective, we can work more readily. Richter offers a helpful elaboration of this point:

> Another [problem with religious, law-based language in ethics] is that it is so imprecise. For instance, if an atheist philosopher argues that abortion is permissible not only are we likely to be thrown by her religious-sounding choice of words, but we also do not know whether by *permissible* she means just, or likely to promote utility, or rational, or what. Anscombe's argument is that such

> philosophers ought instead to use words such as *just*. This way we will have a much better idea what is being said. Judith Jarvis Thomson's famous defense of abortion, for example, makes clear that she is talking about the justice of abortion, whether it violates the rights of the fetus, not whether it is callous or indecent, say. This is the kind of clarification that Anscombe recommends.[23]

In any case, it might seem here that Anscombe is simply defending or promoting a "virtue ethic" rather than LCE. I think to claim this, though, would be premature and unwarranted. She certainly prefers this sort of virtue-based approach to ethics — one that will afford us, as we just noted, richer, more textured descriptions of actions. In a passage of "MMP" that has received a great deal of attention, however, she further discusses the implicit connections between a virtue-based approach to ethics (hereafter VE) and LCE:

> It might remain to look for 'norms' in human virtues: just as *man* has so many teeth, which is certainly not the average number of teeth men have, but is the number of teeth for the species, so perhaps the species *man* regarded not just biologically, but from the point of view of the activity of thought and choice in regard to the various departments of life — powers and faculties and use of things needed — 'has' such-and-such virtues: and this 'man' with the complete set of virtues is the 'norm,' as 'man' with, e.g., a complete set of teeth is the norm. But in *this* sense 'norm' has ceased to be roughly equivalent to 'law.' In *this* sense the notion of a 'norm' brings us nearer to an Aristotelian than a law conception of ethics. There is, I think, no harm in that; but if someone looked in this direction to give 'norm' a sense, then he ought to recognize what has happened to the term 'norm,' which he wanted to mean 'law — without bringing God in': it has ceased to mean 'law' at all; and *so* the expressions 'moral obligation,' 'the moral ought,' and 'duty' are best put on the Index, if he can manage it.[24]

Anscombe seems to be wrestling here with the question of whether VE will afford us normativity, which so concerns modern and contemporary moralists. (She of course, as we have noted, does not seem interested in a sort of special moral normativity the way many of her peers and forbears are and were.) That is, though VE will yield richer, more textured action-descriptions, will it also evoke an appropriate sort of moral force and normativity? There are, it seems, two parts to this response, as I read Anscombe here. First, she seems to think that, following Aristotle, it is quite sufficient to speak of an action as, say, unjust and not further to invoke the fact that it is 'wrong,' in the way that Sidgwick and other contemporary moralists would have us do.[25] This is perhaps yet another restatement of her claim that the search for some sort of special moral normativity is generally misplaced. That being said, she does, as this citation evinces, believe that VE has a certain sort of inherent normativity. What is perhaps most crucial about this normativity, though — at least as she unfolds it here — is that it is distinctly non-ethical; in fact, it is rather more biological in character, though not merely so. She seems in this passage to be referring to a 'man' rather like Aristotle's phronimos, who embodies the collection of virtues the possession of which marks a flourishing human being — a flourishing member of the species homo sapiens. So just as a healthy or fully-equipped man exhibits a certain sort of dental perfection — viz., a full mouth of teeth — so too a healthy, or flourishing man (in a more comprehensive human sense) exhibits various intellectual and affective perfections — chiefly, the moral and intellectual virtues. In this sense, then, Anscombe seems to think that the virtues afford a certain sort of normativity — that they are embodied perfections of the various capacities and faculties of the human being. They are — and the one who embodies them is — something of a golden standard for human constitution and behavior.

She is quick to note, however, that this sort of normativity that the virtues confer is not as such a legal or juridical sort of normativity: i.e., one's failure to embody this or that virtue is not as such the violation of a law, but rather the failure to embody a certain norm of excellence of human constitution and conduct. On the face of things, it is not clear to Anscombe that such a virtue-based norm is law-like — and this seems to trace back to her ongoing concern that law must be promulgated and that natural law is really just (enlightened) rational human participation in eternal divine law. It might be worth considering here, though, an earlier-cited passage of Anscombe's, which deals particularly with the connection between virtues and law on NL/LCE: "To have a law conception of ethics is to hold that what is needed for conformity with the virtues — failure in which is the mark of being bad qua man (and not merely, say qua craftsman of logician) — that what is needed for this, is required by divine law."[26] This passage is important here, I think, because it treats explicitly of the connection, for Anscombe, between the virtues and law. Her crucial point is that, according to LCE, the divine law requires that a man embody the virtues, which are the mark of his being good qua man. (His apprehension of this law and its various precepts might come by way of the natural law, which is his participation in this eternal law by way of reflective human reason, or by supernatural revelation, as contained, say, in holy scripture.) On LCE, the divine law requires, in other words, that man live according to and in fulfillment of "the law of [his] own nature, [which shows] how he must choose to act in matters where his will is free, if his nature is to be properly fulfilled." On this scheme, "[NL] is the proper use of his functions; their misuse or perversion is sin."[27]

According to this picture, with appropriate reflection (and prayer) concerning his constitution and lot in this world, man will appropriately see or realize his need for the virtues — these various excellences of his nature — and, indeed, will see this in a normative, binding sort of way, as perfections to-be-pursued. (This may, of course, require a great deal of help in the form of, say, penance, mortification, and divine grace.) In leading an examined life, as Anscombe reminds us, which the natural law itself fundamentally dictates, man will come to see his need for and acquaint himself with the virtues; and he will come to attune himself to the normative force that they exert on his reflective human conscience, intellect, and will.[28] He will see the claim they have, so to speak, on his life.

One way of reading what Anscombe is doing here is to say that, by focusing her attention on the virtues and related notions of flourishing, for example, she is in fact drawing her readers and interlocutors back to NL/LCE, though not explicitly as such. For she is attuning us to the norms of excellence, the virtues, the possession of which mark our flourishing as human beings. She is thus reacquainting us with what NL and divine law demand of us; but, given our current discourse environment and impoverished and confused notions of moral law, she is doing so through and by appeal to the virtues. She is entering into the heart of the domain of ethics and human action, though by a different (yet complementary) door.

We should be quick here to add that, for Anscombe, such practical-theoretical deliberations about our good, our flourishing as human beings, and the relevant goods or courses of action to pursue are not of themselves — at least not by the work of natural, unaided reason — particularly perspicuous. Moreover, they are, like our ethical discussions in general, in need of revamping at the level of fundamental, foundational concepts and terms. She makes this clear in a summary discussion of a more classical, virtue-based ethical tradition:

> One man — a philosopher — may say that since justice is a virtue, and injustice a vice, and virtues and vices are built up by the performances of the action in which they are instanced, an act of injustice will tend to make a man bad; and essentially the flourishing of a man *qua* man consists in his being good….That is roughly how Plato and Aristotle talk; but it can be seen that philosophically there is a huge gap, at present unfulfillable as far as we are concerned, which needs to be filled by an account of human nature, human action, the type of characteristic a virtue is, and above all of human 'flourishing.' And it is the last concept that appears the most doubtful.[29]

So we have a fundamental predicament, as far as Anscombe is concerned, regarding theoretical discussions of virtues, human flourishing, and related topics. As we have noted throughout the essay, we have the ongoing problem of a vestigial theoretical framework and apparatus from a theistic, Judeo-Christian context whose conceptual and terminological contributions have been more or less eviscerated but are nonetheless employed with mysterious substitute senses and referents. So rather than simply re-articulating a traditional, classical, virtue- (or law-) based ethic, Anscombe asks more basic questions about human nature and constitution, the character of virtues, the concept of 'flourishing' (and related ones), and so on. As the earlier-quoted passages made clear, she does seem to think the whole of ethics to be coextensive with NL, which is simply our participation in the eternal (presumably unchanging) divine law. So it does not seem so much that Anscombe is inviting us to alter our ethical theory profoundly, but rather — particularly given the state of academic and intellectual life — to probe these perennial, fundamental questions anew and in a way that here and now, given our cultural-intellectual inheritance, will do greater justice to and be more beneficial for concepts and theories such as NL/LCE. This seems to be what she is doing in approaching ethics through the clearer, less adulterated lens of the virtues, rather than by the rather muddy waters of moral law.

So we see here from Anscombe something of an ethical program for renewal, to reorient the discipline and move it forth from its current quagmire (that has lasted for some time). First, as we have noted repeatedly, she is in favor of — at least in broader philosophical contexts, and not more narrowly religious or theological ones — laying aside legal/juridical terminology and concepts that came to us through a (Judeo-Christian) religious context and discourse environment that no longer endures. Second, she thinks we do well to return to very fundamental questions that relate to the ethical realm: those of basic philosophical anthropology and conceptual clarification of concepts like the virtues in general or human 'flourishing.' To this list, I think, we can add another noteworthy, related insight: that something of a revised casuistic approach could be quite advantageous. I should clarify what I mean by this, which is something more general than perhaps the typical use of the term 'casuistry.' I simply mean that Anscombe seems to suggest that we can proceed well in ethical deliberation by looking to particular actions, or types of actions, and the virtues and vices associated with them, to illuminate a number of these ethical points of interest. She mentions in passing (in "MMP") that sometimes the best means of shedding light on a particular virtue is simply to look at (alleged) examples of it.[30] We should also note that she followed her own advice in her ethical writings. For she did not produce any single, broadly theoretical topic on ethics (advocating 'virtue ethics,' 'natural law theory,' or anything else). "MMP" seems to have been something of a programmatic piece for her, but her magnum opus was her work *Intention*, which does exactly what she advocates in "MMP": probe a particular piece of the ethical-human-action puzzle, namely intention and intentional action. Some of her other key ethical insights, which I have attempted to highlight herein, are drawn, as we noted, from more particular pieces on sexual or military ethics. Her (unspoken) advice to others seeking to follow suit seems rather clear here: Do not attempt sweeping theoretical work in ethics (and these related disciplines) for the goal of re-articulating traditional natural law theory anew, perhaps in a more contemporary guise. Rather, unpack various key concepts and terms stepwise (e.g., this or that virtue, or perhaps "law" or "obligation" in legal contexts) and also grapple with various "applied" ethical questions (dealing with sex, war, business, or whatever else) to study what seem to be the relevant virtues and vices in those cases. In approaching ethics in this more modest, piecemeal fashion, we can perhaps rediscover and bring back into the fray concepts and ideas that have, down through the years, been lost or obfuscated.

CONSCIENCE: A WAY FORWARD?

Having mined these various insights from Anscombe's texts, I would like to propose a way forward with regard to NL/LCE in particular — one which is broadly reminiscent of, among others, Cardinal Newman. That is, I want to propose a turn or look toward conscience as a means of furthering the NL/LCE project, particularly within an academic philosophical context. I should say a good bit more about what I mean here. We noted that Anscombe ultimately does not seem to despair of NL/LCE as a project; but rather, she seems quite pessimistic about its prospects — when proposed as a normative, law-like approach to ethics — especially within our broader academic and popular culture, which have lost the necessary concomitant notion of divine law. As we also saw, her approach to ethics tends to be rather more virtue-oriented, and she claims that such an approach can yield an appropriate sort of normativity (though not clearly a law-like sort).

I think we can appropriate this reorienting method or plan of Anscombe's to deal with "conscience" as a fundamental ethical (or simply human) concept, much in the manner that she herself has turned our attention (including that of many moral philosophers) back to questions of virtue within ethics. There are several advantages to this move. First, conscience has received scant attention in contemporary philosophical ethics.[31] So it will not likely be a topic — like, say, "ought" and its moral significance — that is fraught with and shrouded in debate, conceptual confusion, and the like. It is relatively untouched in recent philosophical literature — though it was treated rather extensively in the medieval and modern periods. It will, then, afford a point of dialogue with various key periods in the history of philosophy — a methodological point that Anscombe no doubt seems to favor. But treating of conscience will also — perhaps more significantly — offer something of a similar angle on NL/LCE as the virtues and various related concepts did for Anscombe. What I mean by this is that by developing an honest and thorough account of conscience, we will in due course also see the need for a concomitant conception of the natural law, conceived in a manner that will, in my estimation, more or less satisfy the desiderata that we have drawn out from Anscombe's work. Consider how this might work.

Despite the lack of philosophical attention given it of late, conscience is a rather uncontroversial aspect of our ordinary experience of moral reasoning. Most people, that is, can think of instances or situations in which they have felt the prick or pangs of conscience — most often when they have performed some act that they thought they should not have performed or should not have omitted. Indeed, while conscience might be experienced in various ways (as, perhaps, encouraging or forewarning), it is chiefly and arguably most often experienced, in the words of Cardinal Newman, as "a stern monitor."[32] Paradigmatic instances of conscience, that is, involve a sort of prohibition or proscription of certain particular acts and therefore are, as it were, couched imperatively: "Do this," or "don't do that." What is more, such paradigmatic instances of conscience seem to have a discursive or linguistic character to them: that is, they come across as addresses, as though the conscience is speaking a sort of (internal) judgment to the person.[33] Episodes of conscience have the character of being like experiences of judgment issued by another, perhaps even in a judicial sort of context. Kant evinces this aspect in a noteworthy passage from *The Metaphysics of Morals*:

> Every human being has a conscience and finds himself observed, threatened, and, in general, kept in awe (respect coupled with fear) by an internal judge; and this authority watching over the law in him is not something that he himself (voluntarily) *makes*, but something incorporated in his being. It follows him like his shadow when he plans to escape. He can indeed stun himself or put himself to sleep by pleasures and distractions, but he cannot help coming to himself or waking up from time to time; and when he does, he hears at once its fearful voice. He can at most, in extreme depravity, bring himself to *heed* it no longer, but he still cannot help *hearing* it.
>
> Now, this original intellectual and (since it is the thought of duty) moral predisposition called *conscience* is peculiar in that, although its business is a business of a human being with himself, one constrained by his reason sees himself constrained to carry it on as at the bidding *of another person*. For the affair here is that of trying *a case* (*causa*) before a court. But to think of a human being

> who is *accused* by his conscience as *one and the same person* as the judge is an absurd way of representing a court, since then the prosecutor would always lose. For all duties a human being's conscience will, accordingly, have to think of *someone other* than himself (i.e., other than the human being as such) as the judge of his actions, if conscience is not to be in contradiction with itself. This other may be an actual person or a merely ideal person that reason creates for itself.[34]

Kant, then, seems to agree with Newman that conscience serves the role of a sort of severe moral safeguard — one that is rather dogged and relentless in accusing its subject if she does wrong. They would also concur, it seems, that the personal, direct-address character of the injunctions of conscience is noteworthy and deserving of explanation. Newman seems to take this datum as a piece of evidence or argument toward the claim that conscience serves as a sort of voice box for God himself, as it were, to speak personally and intimately into the concrete, practical circumstances of our lives. Kant offers the foregoing difficult account of the personal, direct-address character of the deliverances of conscience — an account that seems ultimately for him (as a clarifying footnote expounds) to involve the necessary postulation of some sort of other self or some sort of hypothetical (human or divine) agent that serves as the personification of conscience's reproving voice. I take it that such a theoretical account is what Anscombe took issue with in Kant for his notion of "self-legislation" in morals and, in particular, in matters of conscience.[35]

Here is where I think we can return quite fruitfully, within such a discussion of conscience, to the topic of NL/LCE. For when we consider the ordinary workings and deliverances of conscience — as we have just (briefly) shown — we rightly recognize them to have (1) a certain strong, normative, imperative character; (2) a direct-address, linguistic sort of delivery that is reminiscent of a personal (even judicial) encounter; and perhaps also (3) a certain unrelenting, persistent manner. We just saw how a Kantian might begin to deal with such data regarding the experience of conscience: by positing or postulating some sort of idealized, internal other self that delivers such judgments. This can perhaps be accomplished by (at least hypothetically) conceiving a sort of mental, interior subdivision of self that enables one to serve as a sort of self-legislator in moral matters. Such a position might be theoretically viable, but it surely seems, on the face of things, to be at least somewhat farfetched and potentially disruptive to one's psychological constitution and integrity (as a moral agent and otherwise). It seems to inveigh against the unity and integrity of the person and introduce into our theorizing a somewhat ad hoc and specious self-distinction.[36]

What I propose in contrast to such a broadly Kantian view of conscience is, in brief, a NL/LCE one, which looks something like this. Episodes of conscience do indeed exhibit (among others) the foregoing three (1-3 above) features, and they do so because such episodes are, in short, concrete applications of various basic, naturally known precepts of the natural law — i.e., of the eternal, divine law of God that is grasped or participated in by means of human reason.[37] The imperative character of the dictates of conscience flows from their being such concrete applications of legal precepts that bind their subjects and, in particular, forbid them from pursuing certain courses of action. Their persistence and enduring character, perhaps, are associated with the fact that such precepts are indeed promulgated laws, the breaking of which appropriately evokes a certain appropriate (nagging) guilt within the offender. And perhaps most importantly, their personal, address-like character stems from the fact that, ultimately, such precepts, as law, issue from a legislator — on a traditional account, the Legislator of all creation who has proscribed various courses of action (and commended so many others) so that his creatures and subjects would be happy, in accordance with his will and governance. In this manner, the precepts of the natural law — which are rational, human participation in the eternal divine law — are themselves utterances, following Cardinal Newman, of God himself that ring out within our souls and consciousness. According to the Judeo-Christian story, these precepts were even personally communicated by God to his people, not just within our rational faculties, so to speak, but on Mount Tabor to Moses, and then fully (according to Christianity) in the person and New Law of Jesus Christ.

CONCLUSION

I have drawn together in this essay various texts of G.E.M. Anscombe that relate to NL and LCE. I have attempted to show that, though she has a fairly traditional view of these matters — and, really, sees them as somehow capturing the whole of ethics — she finds the contemporary discourse, academic and popular, not to be conducive to discussing or invoking them, as certain key aspects of these theories — particularly the necessary notion of divine law — have been, for all intents and purposes, lost or misunderstood. She seems to prefer at present a more virtue-based Aristotelian approach to ethics; and, indeed, she sees such an approach as having certain distinctive virtues, particularly a rich descriptive capacity. She thinks, too, that such an approach can yield a fundamental, authentic sort of ethical normativity, though not perhaps a legal sort, strictly speaking. In drawing on her work, I have contended that, as she found virtue to be a promising, fecund entryway into ethical deliberations, so too could conscience be.[38] It could perhaps also, like virtue, provide a sort of roundabout point of entry back into NL or LCE, particularly as we seek to understand the uniquely personal and persistently imperative character of its deliverances.

NOTES

1. The most noteworthy such essays, to which I will give attention here, are "Address to the Clergy: On Contraception and Natural Family Planning," in *Faith in a Hard Ground: Essays on Religion, Philosophy and Ethics by G.E.M. Anscombe,* ed. Mary Geach and Luke Gormally, vol. 10 in *St. Andrews Studies in Philosophy and Public Affairs,* ed. John Haldane (Exeter: Imprint, 2008),

199-205; "Contraception and Chastity," ibid., 170-191; "Contraception and the Natural Law," *New Blackfriars* 46 (1965): 517-521; "The Justice of the Present War Examined," in *Ethics, Religion, and Politics: Collected Philosophical Papers Volume III* (Oxford: Basil Blackwell, 1981), 72-81; and "Modern Moral Philosophy," in *Human Life, Action, and Ethics: Essays by G.E.M. Anscombe*, ed. Mary Geach and Luke Gormally, vol. 4 in *St. Andrews Studies in Philosophy and Public Affairs* (Exeter: Imprint, 2005), 169-194.

2. Anscombe, "Justice," 72-73.
3. Anscombe, "Contraception and Chastity," 179.
4. Anscombe, "Natural Law," 517.
5. Ibid., 518.
6. See notes 2 and 3.
7. It seems that a potential point of criticism drawing on this line of thought from Anscombe is that certain contemporary formulations of natural law theory tend too much in the direction of stressing, e.g., the primacy of various basic goods and so lose the chiefly *legal* aspect of NL. It becomes hard to see, in other words, if one leans too heavily on such an approach, how exactly the natural law is *law* in a primary way. I do not have the space here to look at any particular theories to this effect. It is worth noting, however, that at least several authors seem to have registered a similar concern. See, e.g., Fulvio Di Blasi, *God and the Natural Law: A Rereading of Thomas Aquinas* (South Bend: St. Augustine's Press, 2002); Russell Hittinger, *The First Grace: Rediscovering Natural Law in a Post-Christian World* (Wilmington: Intercollegiate Studies Institute, 2007), especially chapter 2; and Jeremy Waldron, "What is Natural Law Like," in *Reason, Morality, and Law: The Philosophy of John Finnis*, ed. John Keown and Robert P. George (Oxford: Oxford University Press, 2014), 73-92.
8. See note 5 and Anscombe, "Address to the Clergy," 200.
9. Anscombe, "MMP," 169.
10. Duncan Richter, e.g., devoted an entire book to ethics in the wake of this groundbreaking essay. See his *Ethics after Anscombe: Post "Modern Moral Philosophy*," vol. 5 in *Library of Ethics and Applied Philosophy* (Dordrecht: Kluwer, 2000).
11. Her magnum opus, which treats of intentional action — and so of philosophical psychology more generally — is *Intention* (Cambridge, MA: Harvard University Press, 2000).
12. "MMP," 176.
13. Ibid., 179-180.
14. Ibid., 171.
15. Ibid., 180.
16. Ibid., 187.
17. See note 13.
18. Duncan Richter, "G.E.M. Anscombe," *Internet Encyclopedia of Philosophy*, accessed September 20, 2014, http://www.iep.utm.edu/anscombe/. This sort of insistence from Anscombe on a lost tradition, framework, or environment for dialogue and discourse regarding topics such as moral law seems to anticipate the project of Alasdair MacIntyre, particularly in *After Virtue: A Study in Moral Theory* (South Bend: University of Notre Dame Press, 1981).
19. Anscombe published "Contraception and Natural Law," for instance, as a reply to Herbert McCabe, a Dominican priest colleague, in the Dominicans' *New Blackfriars* journal.
20. See notes 3 and 4.

21. She might therefore, to echo comments in note 7, have concerns about natural law theories that attempt rather decisively to identify the natural law more simply with norms of reasonableness or various basic goods. In other words, she seems particularly keen on the natural law's being rational, human participation in the eternal, divine law — the latter part of which we cannot forget or exclude in our theoretical accounts.

22. See note 13.
23. Richter, "Anscombe."
24. "MMP," 188.
25. Ibid., 190.
26. See note 12.
27. See note 2.
28. See note 4.
29. "MMP," 193.
30. Ibid., 190.

31. Conscience was of course a lively topic for high and late medieval thinkers such as Aquinas, Bonaventure, Scotus, and Ockham, as well as for modern authors like Kant, Locke, and Butler. It does not, however, seem to be of particular interest in more recent philosophical ethics. See, e.g., how the principal entry in the *Stanford Encyclopedia of Philosophy* dealing with conscience concerns *medieval* theories of it, rather than the notion of conscience more broadly. (See Douglas Langston, "Medieval Theories of Conscience," *Stanford Encyclopedia of Philosophy*, accessed September 20, 2014, http://plato.stanford.edu/entries/conscience-medieval/.) John Cottingham has made a commendable recent attempt to reintroduce conscience into contemporary philosophical debate. See his "'Our Natural Guide . . .': Conscience, 'Nature', and Moral Experience" in *Human Values: New Essays on Ethics and Natural Law*, ed. David S. Oderberg and Timothy Chappell (Basingstoke: Palgrave Macmillan, 2004), 11-31.

32. John Henry Newman, "Letter to the Duke of Norfolk," sec. 5, para. 246, accessed October 20, 2014, http://www.newmanreader.org/works/anglicans/volume2/gladstone/section5.html.

33. Paul Strohm notes this feature of conscience and describes it as a "still lingering" question with regard to "conscience's visitations." See his *Conscience: A Very Short Introduction* (Oxford: Oxford University Press, 2011), 101.

34. Immanuel Kant, *The Metaphysics of Morals*, ed. Mary Gregor (Cambridge: Cambridge University Press, 1996), 189.

35. See note 14.

36. Adam Smith seems to have been a predecessor to Kant in developing such a curious, arguably schizophrenic view of conscience. For more on this, see Strohm, *Conscience*, 48-49.

37. I take the basic contours of this sort of account to be broadly Thomistic, following the general scheme articulated by Aquinas in *Summa Theologica* I, Q. 79, Art. 12-13, trans. Fathers of the English Dominican Province (New York: Benzinger Brothers, 1947). Newman articulates a similar account of the particularity of conscience with respect to concrete acts in "Letter;" and Strohm commends such a broadly Thomistic account in *Conscience*.

38. I am grateful to Walter Raubicheck and two anonymous readers for *Lex Naturalis*, who all encouraged me to revise and substantiate this final section and argument of the essay.

ARS LEGIS: REFLECTIONS ON AQUINAS' "CHRISTIAN" ARTICULATION OF THE NATURAL AND HUMAN LAW

Jeffrey Walkey

With the exception of the *quinque viae*, the most commented upon questions of the *Summa Theologiae* of Thomas Aquinas are likely those on law (*ST* I-II, qq. 90-108). Interestingly, however, many expositions and translations of these questions cover only part of Aquinas' discussion.[1] More specifically, scholars have often confined their considerations of law in Aquinas to qq. 90-97 (i.e., law in itself, eternal law, natural law, and human law) in isolation from qq. 98-108 (i.e., Divine law—Old and New). This restriction might appear justified, at least, on the practical grounds that qq. 90-97 are less obviously theological, and likely considered more relevant and more palatable in the public square. Such an approach to Aquinas' treatment of law, then, is thought by many to have provided a philosophical account of natural (and human) law, one that articulates a universally accessible ground from which Christians and non-Christians might continue a dialogue concerning normative ethics and the ordering of the public or social sphere.

Critics argue, however, that Aquinas cannot be thought to have proposed a strictly philosophical account of natural law, because the "treatise" itself is articulated within a work of Christian theology by a Christian theologian for a Christian audience. That is to say, the account assumes the special revelation and context of Christian faith, in which the natural law is Christologically determined, as rooted in the eternal law, namely, the Word of God; and as such, Aquinas' account of natural law does not propose a universally accessible ground for normative ethics and the ordering of the public sphere.

Against such objections, while granting the specifically Christian character of the "treatise," I argue that Aquinas' intention is nonetheless to present an account of natural law in which its principles and determinations are universally accessible. Rather than argue in favor of this relatively common interpretation directly by recourse to this or that passage within the *Summa Theologiae*, I will, instead, do so indirectly, by shedding light on Aquinas' account by means of a comparison between natural law and the art of "building dwellings." Ultimately, just as the knowledge and virtue (*ars*) necessary to the art of building were and are attainable before and after the Incarnation, so too the knowledge and virtue (*prudentia*) necessary to the art of law. The impetus for this particular comparison comes from Aquinas himself. In *ST* I-II, q. 109, a. 2, co., he states, "[B]ecause human nature is not altogether corrupted by sin, so as to be shorn of every natural good, even in the state of corrupted nature it can, by virtue of its natural endowments, work some particular good, as to building dwellings, plant vineyards, and the like."[2] The relevance of this comparison becomes more obvious in light of Aquinas' repeated references to the parallel between speculative and practical reasoning, on the one hand, and the processes involved in art, on the other.[3]

Building dwellings can be and in fact is the kind of thing about which Christians and non-Christians can intelligibly reason together. That is to say, even in the postlapsarian condition and apart from the special revelation of God in Christ and the grace of faith, according to Aquinas, human beings have the capacity to know the principles and make the determinations necessary to attain to the particular good of building dwellings well. This claim appears indisputable. That Aquinas makes such claims in a work of Christian theology as a Christian theologian for a specifically Christian audience does not detract from nor does it negate the universality of those claims. In other words, Aquinas' Christian faith does nothing to undermine or negate his intention to say something universal about human nature's capacities apart from the special revelation of God in Christ. Similarly, then, in light of the comparison he makes, Aquinas' claims about the universal accessibility of the principles and determinations of natural law are by no means undermined or negated by his Christian faith and specifically Christian aims. That is to say, natural law—and by extension, human law—is, according to Aquinas, the kind of thing about which Christians and non-Christians can intelligibly reason together. If the analogy holds, on Thomistic grounds the contention that the capacity to know and reason about the principles and determinations of natural law only obtain within or, at least, subsequent to the graced context of Christian faith, rooted in the special revelation of God in Christ, is no more true for Aquinas than to suggest that the capacity to know and reason about the principles and determinations of the art of building dwellings only obtain within or subsequent to the graced context of Christian faith.

To this end, the discussion that follows will be threefold: (1) I will briefly describe the principles and processes of the art of building, its relationship to the eternal law, and the requisite determinations involved in building well; (2) I will briefly articulate the broad outlines of Aquinas' account of natural law, its relationship to eternal law, and its determinations in human and divine law; and lastly, (3), having articulated each of these, I will highlight the ways in which these two articulations are structurally parallel, and that, insofar as the former is a natural capacity of human nature *qua* human nature, apart from the grace of special revelation and faith in Christ, so too, is the latter. Ultimately, then, even though Aquinas is a Christian theologian writing a work of Christian theology for a Christian audience, his account of natural law and its determinations in human law is intended to name what is in principle universally accessible to all human beings, "[a]t all times and among all nations."[4] Much like the art of building, the principles and determinations of natural law in human law are the kind of thing about which Christians and non-Christians can intelligibly reason together for the sake of ordering the shared social and public sphere.

THE ART OF BUILDING AND THE RE-ORDERING OF GRACE

In his discussion of the necessity of grace (*ST* I-II, q. 109), Aquinas draws our attention to the various kinds of goods attainable by virtue of the natural endowments of human nature *qua* human nature. On the one hand, he observes that human beings, had they not fallen into sin, were capable of attaining certain goods which were "proportionate to his nature" (*suae naturae proportionatum*), for instance, acquired virtue.[5] By means of the grace of faith in Christ, on the other hand, which heals and elevates nature, human beings could attain certain goods that surpass their natural capacities, for example, the merit of supernatural beatitude.[6] Unfortunately, because of the sin of our first parents, our natural capacities are subject to failure. That is to say, the effects of sin hinder the natural capacity of human nature to attain many of the goods otherwise attainable. Yet, Aquinas maintains, in spite of our postlapsarian condition, that human beings remain capable of certain proportionate goods, such as "to build dwellings, plant vineyards, and the like."[7]

In light of this claim, let us consider the sorts of things we do in fact know and achieve with respect to, for example, the art of building apart from the grace of faith.[8] And then, having done so, it will be important to consider how the special graces of Christian revelation and faith affect and re-order such natural capacities, affecting considerations of both the relevant ends and forms. Articulating the principles and determinations involved in the art of building will provide us with the analogy, or rather the lens, through which to approach considerations of Aquinas' account of natural law, its principles, forms, ends, and particular determinations, especially as they relate to the specifications of human law and the New Law of grace brought by Christ.

Like other arts, building proceeds from certain general principles, with particular determinations of those principles, according to a form appropriately specified in light of the end(s) sought. Regarding the first, we observe that, just as the speculative reason proceeds from first principles to particular conclusions, so also does the art of building proceed from general principles to particular determinations in the concrete.[9] Yet, the general principles of building, unlike those of speculative reason and natural law, are not instilled in human nature, but rather must be discovered through observing the physical (and chemical) laws that obtain in our universe.

They are nonetheless, like the first principles of speculative reason and the basic principles of the natural law, rooted in the Divine Reason. That is to say, much like the principles of speculative and practical reasoning, the physical and chemical laws of the universe participate in the eternal law. Each being, as the kind of being that it is, participates in the ordering of the universe by God in the manner appropriate to that being. Aquinas observes, "[A]ll actions and movements of the whole of nature are subject to the eternal law. Consequently, irrational creatures are subject to the eternal law, through being moved by Divine providence."[10]

As created beings of a particular kind, each behaves—that is to say, each "acts" and "moves"—in accordance with eternal law. Material beings, for instance, if left unobstructed, tend to move toward the center of its gravitation field. The builder, in order to produce the desired structure, must account for such "natural laws," insofar as they aid or hinder achieving the end sought. Thus, insofar as a builder wishes to construct a sturdy product, she must recognize that stronger materials withstand more force, bear more weight, and are to be preferred. Similarly, she must recognize that the integrity of (most) materials weakens over longer expanses. Further, plumbing and HVAC[11] systems, in order to achieve the desired efficiency, must take account of the fact that water flows "downhill" and heat rises. More generally, the principles of mathematics are crucial for drafting and design, estimating and purchasing, as well as land surveying and measuring in the field. Each of these is rather simple, possibly obvious; and each is rooted in the eternal law. More importantly, for our purposes, each of these principles is knowable apart from the special revelation of God in Christ, to believer and non-believer alike. Although in the "order of being," the Logos, who is the

Second Person of the Trinity, through whom the world is created, is prior (ontologically), nonetheless, in the "order of knowing," the relevant principles obtain and are knowable apart from knowledge of the Logos as incarnate in Jesus of Nazareth.

In order to build a dwelling well, then, one must proceed according to principles of this sort, which are, again, rooted in the eternal law. Yet, such general principles must be applied appropriately given concrete circumstances. That is to say, the general principles must be determined or specified according to the particularities of this or that project. Where are we building? What materials are required? Is it better to use timber or steel to carry the load of certain walls? Or, how best can we anchor the foundation given this or that particular plot of land?

Many determinations of this sort are made in light of a specific form according to which and end for which the builder exercises her craft. Is the desired building a business center? Are there certain medical and technological requirements, as in the case of hospitals or assisted-living facilities? Decisions regarding the proper form a building must take cannot be made apart from considerations of the particular end for which the dwelling is being built. One might build for the sake of self-preservation, or build to provide for his household, or even for the sake of the art itself. In the end, all determinations of this kind can be adequately—and, often, exceptionally—discerned and implemented apart from the special revelation brought in Christ, by believers and non-believers alike.

What difference, then, does the grace of Christian revelation and faith make to the art of building? As noted, builders build for the sake of certain ends. The excellence of this or that building project will be, at least in part, measured in light of such ends. Further, in most cases, the end sought in the art of building remains ordered to particular earthly realities, such as survival, convenience, or aesthetics. Grace, though utilizing the very same principles and requiring the same practical virtues, re-orders one's consideration of ends, directing them beyond immanent ends simply to a transcendent end, namely, to the love of God.

Consider the following example. A prospective owner may be an extraordinarily wealthy individual, with numerous properties, who desires a new home for the sake of vanity or luxury. Grace, which is ordered to the love of God and neighbor, might determine the builder's actions in such a way that she chooses not to build such a home. The builder could construct the home, and excel in doing so, which would be a good in itself. In the order of charity, however, for the love of God and neighbor, the builder might discern that building an unnecessary, lavish home for persons who do not need such housing is poor stewardship, potentially serving vanity rather than the good. In light of the Gospel, enlivened by grace, the builder might restrict the availability of her services based on, for instance, an option for the poor and the homeless. Similarly, the builder might be entirely competent to build extraordinarily elegant, sophisticated housing. Yet, in the order of charity, stewardship might call for simplicity and efficient use of space for the sake of housing more people. Moreover, ecological and environmental stewardship might call for the refusal to build in certain "profitable" areas for the sake of creation itself. The list could go on.

Although grace elevates and re-orders considerations of ends, and as such further determines the forms and principles of the art of building, it is significant that grace does so while maintaining and employing the natural capacities of human nature as such. Building that is ordered by charity does not reject the general principles of building, nor many of its more immediate determinations, but further determines them. It does not neglect the particular determinations of this or that locale, this or that project, but rather further specifies them in service to God and neighbor. As such, building that is ordered by charity does not negate the natural immanent principles and ends of the art of building, but rather perfects them by elevating them. Nevertheless, in spite of the re-ordering of grace, the principles and requisite skills, those necessary to the art of building well in light of the chosen end, are attainable by the Christian and non-Christian alike.

The observations thus far have shown that human beings have a natural capacity for knowing and determining the principles, forms, and ends of building. Although potentially elevated and reordered by grace, quite simply, with respect to the art of building — that is to say, of the ability to build well — the non-Christian is on equal footing with the Christian. Even though the physical and chemical laws with which the builder must work are, according to Aquinas, rooted in the eternal law, which is the Divine Reason, this specifically theological and Christological ground of such principles does nothing to undermine the universal accessibility of those principles. In the "order of being," so to speak, indeed, God, and the Word as the eternal law, is the ground upon which the physical and chemical laws of nature rest. In the "order of knowing," however, it is clear that specifically Christian considerations need not precede or accompany excellence in the art of building. These are things most of us do in fact believe. Most of us do not ask our builders or plumbers or carpenters whether they are Christian before soliciting their services, because, with respect to such things, the special grace of revelation and faith in Christ are not uniquely determinative with respect to the principles and secondary determinations considered in light of the chosen ends.

As we move on to the discussion of law and grace in Aquinas, we should keep these things in mind. Given the parallel he often draws between speculative and practical reasoning and art, and especially in light of his claim that building is, in fact, something human beings remain capable of doing despite sin and apart from the special revelation and the grace of faith in Christ (see *ST* I-II, q. 109, a. 2, co.), it will be important to see how his account of law and grace unfolds in a similar manner. Let us turn to this now.

AQUINAS, LAW, AND THE RE-ORDERING OF GRACE

Aquinas defines law as "an ordinance of reason for the common good, made by him who has care of the community, and promulgated."[12] Restated, to be a law, a measure or rule must be in accord with reason, directed toward the good of the whole community, and be promulgated by someone with the authority to do so. Household rules, civil laws, and the like, to the extent that they conform to this definition, each has the character of law. More importantly, however, a measure has the character of law, for Aquinas, to the extent that it participates in the eternal law, which, again, is the Divine Reason.

The eternal law, as law, must be promulgated. Promulgation occurs in different ways: by word and in nature. With respect to the laws of nature, which govern the acts and movements of all beings, the primary means by which the eternal law is promulgated to and participated in is through each being's nature. Divine Reason, which is Providence, governs all things, rational and irrational, animate and inanimate, by imprinting upon them specific inclinations "to their proper acts and ends."[13] In the case of rational creatures, God endowed nature with the capacity to participate in the eternal law in a "most excellent way" (*excellentiori quodam modo*) through the use of reason.[14] Aquinas states, "The natural law is promulgated by the very fact that God instilled it [i.e., the natural law] into man's mind so as to be known by him."[15] It is important to emphasize, that, for Aquinas, this instillation of the natural law and the knowledge of its precepts is universal, obtaining from the moment of creation, and in this case, the creation of human beings.[16] Just as the first principles of speculative reason are self-evident, but only to those who have both the time and acumen to grasp them, the precepts of natural law are naturally (potentially) knowable by all human beings *qua* human.[17]

The foundational principle of natural law for rational creatures, from which the others are derived, is the precept to seek good and avoid evil.[18] Aquinas argues, "[G]ood has the nature of an end, and evil, the nature of a contrary, hence it is that all things to which man has a natural inclination, are naturally apprehended by reason as being good, and consequently as objects of pursuit, and their contraries as evil, and objects of avoidance."[19] The primary principles of the natural law, then, include this basic principle to seek the good, as well as those precepts which follow immediately therefrom.

Among the specific goods to be sought, about which certain immediate precepts of the natural law pertain, Aquinas lists self-preservation, procreation, life in society, and knowledge of the truth about God. He notes, for example, "every substance seeks the preservation of its own being, according to its nature: and by reason of this inclination, whatever is a means of preserving human life, and of warding off its obstacles, belongs to the natural law."[20] The inclination to self-preservation, which flows from the basic principle to seek what is good, as a general principle of the natural law, entails further specifications in light of particular circumstances and particular natures. Such secondary determinations are made in two ways. First, they can be derived as "demonstrated conclusions are drawn from the principles" in the speculative sciences.[21] Aquinas offers "one must not kill" as an example of the first way. One can determine from the general principles of practical reasoning, as conclusion from premises, that killing (or harming) another is contrary to the natural law. He observes, insofar as laws of this kind are found in human law, "[they] are contained in human law not as emanating therefrom exclusively, but have some force from the natural law."[22] Secondly, Aquinas suggests that the secondary determinations of natural law, as they appear in, for instance, human law, are also derived as a craftsman determines "the general form of a house" in light of circumstances.[23] He notes, for instance, that evil ought to be punished (*the general principle*), but the specification of this or that punishment for particular evils (*the determination*) is more like the determination of form by a craftsman than conclusions drawn from premises by the speculative reason. As such, then, these determinations of the natural law "have no other force than that of human law."[24]

The particular determinations prescribed in human law are made and promulgated within particular circumstances of this or that community, taking a specific form in light of a particular end. According to Aquinas, the end of human law is "the temporal tranquility of the state, which end law effects by directing external actions."[25] It is concerned primarily with justice between human beings and human communities. The end of human law, then, which is an immanent end, seeks to foster virtue for the good of the community through certain determinations of external acts. These determinations are ordered together in various ways, various forms, in light of the various contingencies, contributing to the ordering of the social and public sphere. Although grounded in and derived from its principles, human law does not regulate all that the natural law contains. As Aquinas suggests, "The purpose of human law is to lead men to virtue, not suddenly, but gradually."[26] Different persons find themselves in different states with respect to virtue and goodness. Thus, human law must be tailored in such a way to bring about positive transformation, without stunting development through overburdening. He notes, "[S]ince the same thing is not possible to one who has not a virtuous habit, as is possible to one who has…many things are permissible to men not perfect in virtue, which would be intolerable in a virtuous man."[27] In light of the end of human law, which is justice and the good of the community, the principles of natural law must be determined in human law so that the public sphere is formed in such a way that this end is attained.

So, what of grace? Aquinas offers four reasons for the necessity of Divine law. First, the final end for which human beings have been created is beyond the reach of natural capacities. If human beings were not called beyond the immanent end of a just social order, or virtuous action proportionate to natural capacities, the natural law and our capacity to make particular determinations in human law would be sufficient. As it stands, however, humans are called to partake in the Divine life, to live beyond nature and its capacities. Thus, the Divine law was given that human beings might be properly ordered to their final, higher end.[28] Second, the Divine law is given for the sake of certitude, the greatest certitude, rooted in God's authority as lawgiver. Human judgment can be mistaken, especially, in particular determinations of law. Aquinas suggests, "In order, therefore, that man may know without doubt what he ought to do and what he ought to avoid, it was necessary for man to be directed… by a law given by God."[29] Third, the final end of human existence is the transcendent, supernatural end of the vision of God. This end, which implies a "perfection of virtue," requires right internal acts as well as right external acts.[30] Internal acts fall outside the competence of the natural as determined in human law. As Aquinas observes, "[M]an is not competent to judge of interior movements that are hidden, but only of exterior acts which appear."[31] Yet human laws derived from natural law are intended and competent to order external acts to immanent ends. Thus, it was necessary that God intervene, not only directing human actions to a higher end, but also directing both the internal and external acts to that end. Fourth, as noted above, human law does not legislate against all evil acts but "only the more grievous vices" (*sed solum graviora*).[32] Such "less" grievous evils, however, must be punished and rooted out. In order that all evil, internal and external, more and less grievous, might be punished, God has provided the Divine law, which legislates against such acts. Aquinas says, "In order, therefore, that no evil might remain unforbidden and unpunished, it was necessary for the Divine law to supervene, whereby all sins are forbidden."[33]

Aquinas makes a further distinction between two kinds of Divine law, namely, the Old and the New. The Old law primarily refers to the Decalogue and other precepts of the Mosaic Law. Such precepts, although containing all the precepts of the natural law, legislate above and beyond the natural law. Ordered to a higher end, the Old law further determines the natural law beyond the specification of human law, calling for those acts prescribed in Jewish law. As Aquinas notes, "[T]he precepts of the natural law are general, and require to be determined: and they are determined both by human law and by Divine law."[34] The Old law, then, is subsequent to the natural law, further determining and specifying the precepts of the natural law, re-ordering them to a higher end.

Although the Old law further determines the natural law and human law, ordering human existence to a higher end, it was insufficient. Merely providing "some assistance,"[35] the Old law needed further determination and supplementation. Aquinas argues, "Man cannot fulfill all the precepts of the law, unless he fulfill the precept of charity…Consequently it is not possible… for man to fulfill the law without grace."[36] Law, then, as ordered to the supernatural end of beatitude, must be further determined by the law of grace, which is the New Law. This law is promulgated both in writing and in our hearts through the infusion of grace. One receives this grace "through God's Son made man."[37] This "law of love"[38] informs human acts with charity, determining them through elevation, in order that the law is perfectly fulfilled (externally and internally) out of love rather than fear of punishment.

This account of the natural law and the further determinations of human and Divine law have revealed a process from first principles to mediating determinations and further to supernatural determinations. The inclinations and precepts of the natural law (general principles) are particularized in details by human law (determinations), and those determinations are ordered with a certain telos (end) according to a certain type (form). The Divine law further determines the natural and human law, first with respect to external acts (i.e., the Old law), and then with respect to internal acts (i.e., the New law). These laws direct human action to a higher end, re-ordering them to the love of God and neighbor. The Divine laws neither negate nor merely duplicate the precepts of the natural law, but rather often affirm and elevate such precepts. Not surprisingly, these processes are very similar to those already articulated above, with respect to the art of building. In the last section, I will highlight the parallels further, as well as drawing out the implications of this analogy.

THE ART OF LAW: RÉSUMÉ

At the beginning of this essay, I noted certain objections to the common extraction of Aquinas' treatment of natural law from its specifically Christian context. Citing Fergus Kerr and D. Stephen Long, I indicated that such reductively philosophical renderings of Aquinas' account of law treats what is theologically and Christologically determined as though it were not. Natural law for Aquinas, according to this position, must be read within the broader context of his treatment of law and grace, that is to say, the eternal and natural law together with his considerations of the Old and New (Divine) Law. Aquinas was a Christian theologian writing a work of Christian theology for a Christian audience. Moreover, his account of the principles of natural law are explicitly rooted in the eternal law, which is the Word, that is to say, the Second Person of the Trinity, through whom the world came to be.

All of this is to be granted. Aquinas is writing as a Christian for Christians, with specifically Christian aims. This is true, and this is significant. It is significant, however, not because it as such undermines or negates the universal accessibility of the natural law. Rather, it is significant because from within this work of Christian theology we encounter a Christian theologian arguing that the principles of the natural law, which are rooted in the eternal law of the Triune God, are universally accessible to human beings *qua* human, "[a]t all times and among all nations."[39]

This becomes clear in light of the analogy between law and the art of building. Art, and specifically the art of "building dwellings," is described from within a Christian context by a Christian thinker. The principles upon which the art of building depend, namely, the physical and chemical laws of nature, are, like the natural law, rooted in the eternal law, which is the Logos, the Word of God. In the order of knowing, however, those principles upon which building depends can be and in fact are recognized and determined in the various processes of construction by a vast number of individuals, believers and non-believers alike. And again, Aquinas himself explicitly identifies "building dwellings" as one of those proportionate goods attainable by human nature corrupted by sin, and apart from the special revelation of God in Christ and the grace of faith.

Consequently, in light of the analogy between law and the art of building, we have cause to affirm, on Thomistic grounds, that the knowledge and determinations of the principles of natural law, which are rooted in the eternal law, is, like the art of building, something about which Christians and non-Christians might profitably reason together. Speaking as a Christian, from within a specifically

Christian context, Aquinas affirms the universal accessibility and natural capacity of human beings *qua* human to know and determine the principles of natural law "[a]t all times and among all nations."[40] In the end, the very analogy itself between law and the art of building might indicate that the dialogue will work itself out much more like an organic collaboration between artists than by means of the analyses of philosophers. In this sense, Aquinas seems to have articulated what amounts to the *art of law*, rather than a science.

NOTES

1. These include, for instance, *St. Thomas on Politics and Ethics: A Norton Critical Edition*, trans. Paul Sigmund (New York: W.W. Norton and Company, 1988); *Thomas Aquinas: Selected Philosophical Writings*, trans. Timothy McDermott (Oxford: Oxford University Press, 1993); *Treatise on Law*, intro. Ralph McInerny (Washington: Regnery Publishing, 1996); *Readings in Christian Ethics: A Historical Sourcebook*, ed. J. Philip Wogaman (Louisville: Westminster John Know Press, 1996). Of course, there are exceptions, e.g., Fergus Kerr and Alfred Freddoso.

2. *ST* I-II, q. 109, a. 2, co.: "Quia tamen natura humana per peccatum non est totaliter corrupta, ut scilicet toto bono naturae privetur; potest quidem etiam in statu naturae corruptae, per virtutem suae naturae aliquid bonum particulare agere, sicut aedificare domos, plantare vineas, et alia huiusmodi."

3. See *ST* I-II, q. 90, a. 1, ad 2; q. 94, a. 1, co.; q. 94, a. 2, s.c. and co. Cf. *ST* I-II, q. 93, a. 1, co.; q. 95, a. 2, co.; q. 95, a. 3, co.

4. *ST* II-II, q. 85, a. 1, s.c.

5. See *ST* I-II, q. 109, a. 2, co.

6. For a helpful treatment of Aquinas on grace, specifically as it relates to merit, see Joseph P. Wawrykow, *God's Grace and Human Action: 'Merit' in the Theology of Thomas Aquinas* (Notre Dame: University of Notre Dame Press, 1995).

7. *ST* I-II, q. 109, a. 2, co.: "…aedificare domos, plantare vineas, et alia huiusmodi."

8. Although the author has a background in residential construction, much of what follows remains nothing more than an informed layperson's account of the process.

9. See *ST* I-II, q. 90, a. 1, ad 2; q. 94, a. 1, co.; q. 94, a. 2, s.c.and co. Concerning the analogy between law and art, see *ST* I-II, q. 93, a. 1, co.; q. 95, a. 2, co.: "[I]t must be noted that something may be derived from the natural law in two ways…the second mode is likened to that whereby, in the arts, general forms are particularized as to details: thus the craftsman needs to determine the general form of a house to some particular shape (Sed sciendum est quod a lege

naturali dupliciter potest aliquid derivari...Secundo vero modo simile est quod in artibus formae communes determinantur ad aliquid special, sicut artifex formam commune domus necesse est quod determinet ad hanc vel illam domus figuram)." Cf. *ST* I-II, q. 95, a. 3, co.

10. *ST* I-II, q. 93, a. 5, co.: "Et per hanc etiam rationem omnes motus et actiones totius naturae legi aeternae subduntur. Unde alio modo creaturae irrationals subduntur legi aeternae, inquantum moventur a divina providential." See, also, *ST* I-II, q. 93, a. 5, ad 1: "The impression of an inward principle is to natural things, what the promulgation of law is to men ([Q]uod hoc modo se habet impressio activi prinicipii intrinseci, quantum ad res naturales, sicut se habet promulgation legis quantum ad homines)." Cf. *ST* I-II, q. 93, a. 1, co.

11. This is an industry acronym which means "Heating, Ventilation, and Air Conditioning."

12. *ST* I-II, q. 90, a. 4, co.: "[Definitio legi] nihil est aliud quam quaedam rationis ordinatio ad bonum commune, ab eo qui curam communitatis habet, promulgata."

13. *ST* I-II, q. 91, a. 2, co.: "...in proprios actus et fines."

14. *ST* I-II, q. 91, a. 2, co. Cf. *Summa Contra Gentiles* III, 111, 1.

15. *ST* I-II, q. 90, a. 4, ad 1: "[P]romulgatio legis naturae est ex hoc ipso quod Deus eam mentibus hominum inseruit naturaliter cognoscendam." See, also, q. 91, a. 2, co.: "...the light of natural reason, whereby we discern what is good and evil, which is the function of the natural law, is nothing else than an imprint on us of the Divine light (...quasi lumen rationis naturalis, quo discernimus quid sit bonum et malum, quod pertinent ad naturalem legem, nihil aliud sit quam impression divini luminis in nobis)"; Cf. q. 94, a. 1, s.c.; q. 94, a. 4, s.c. A similar position seems implied in q. 99, a. 2, ad 1 and q. 106, a. 1, ad 2.

16. See *ST* I-II, q. 94, a. 1, s.c. Cf. *ST* II-II, q. 85, a. 1, s.c. This is a disputed claim, one that this essay seeks to address, at least, in part. For the moment, note that the precepts are rooted in the inclinations of a natural form as individuated in particular human beings. Those inclinations are not unknown prior to Incarnation, only to be revealed by the special revelation and faith brought by Christ. Rather, the inclinations and corresponding precepts are more or less known by natural endowments. This is not to say that human nature is in any sense *complete* apart from this grace, but rather to suggest that it is *competent* to know and perform certain things apart from it, among them, to know and determine the principles of natural law in human law.

17. *ST* I-II, q. 94, a. 2, co.: "[T]he precepts of the natural law are to the practical reason, what the first principles of demonstrations are to the speculative reason; because both are self-evident principles....But some propositions are self-evident only to the wise ([P]raecepta legis naturae hoc modo se habent ad rationem practicam, sicut principia prima demonstrationum se habent ad rationem speculativam, utraque enim sunt quaedam principia per se nota)."

18. This is to say that the human will tends toward happiness as to an end, but always under the aspect of the good. See, for instance, *ST* I, q. 82, aa. 1-3 and I-II, q. 1, aa. 1-6. Cf. *ScG* III, 3, 2: "Now, that toward which an agent tends in a definite way must be appropriate to it, because the agent would not be inclined to it except by virtue of some agreement with it. But, what is appropriate to something is good for it. So, every agent acts for a good." Also, *De veritate* q. 22, a. 1, s.c. and a. 1, ad 4, "When we say that all things tend to good, good is not to be restricted to this or that but to be taken in its generality, because each being naturally tends to a good suitable to itself."

19. *ST* I-II, q. 94, a. 2, co.: "[B]onum habet rationem finis, malum autem rationem contrarii, inde est quod omnia illa ad quae homo habet naturalem inclinationem, ratio naturaliter apprehendit ut bona, et per consequens ut opere prosequenda, et contraria eorum ut mala et vitanda."

20. *ST* I-II, q. 94, a. 2, co.: "[P]rout scilicet quaelibet substantia appetit conservationem sui esse secundum suam naturam. Et secundum hanc inclinationem, pertinent ad legem naturalem ea per quae vita hominis conservatur, et contrarium impeditur."

21. *ST* I-II, q. 95, a. 2, co.: "...ex principiis conclusiones demonstrativae producuntur."

22. *ST* I-II, q. 95, a. 2, co.: "...continentur lege humana non tanquam sint solum lege posita, sed habent etiam aliquid vigoris ex lege naturalis."

23. *ST* I-II, q. 95, a. 2, co.: "...formam commune domus."

24. *ST* I-II, q. 95, a. 2, co.: "...ex sola lege humana vigorem habent."

25. *ST* I-II, q. 98, a. 1, co.: "Legis enim humanae finis est temporalis tranquillitas civitatis, ad quem finem pervenit lex cohibendo exteriors actus."

26. *ST* I-II, q. 96, a. 2, ad 2: "[L]ex humana intendit homines inducer ad virtutem, non subito, sed gradatim."

27. *ST* I-II, q. 96, a. 2, co.: "...non enim idem est possibile ei qui non habet habitum virtutis, et virtuoso...sunt permittenda hominibus non perfectis virtute, quae non essent toleranda in hominibus virtuosis."

28. Note that Aquinas is not arguing that the Divine law is necessary that the natural law may be known, but rather in order that human beings may be directed beyond nature to its true final end. Knowledge of the precepts of the natural law is not a latent capacity which must be excited by and function within the Divine law, but rather, it is a natural capacity of human nature (as such) which is sufficient for the proportionate immanent ends.

29. *ST* I-II, q. 91, a. 4, co.: "Ut ergo homo absque omni dubitatione scire possit quid ei sit agendum et vitandum, necessarium fuit ut in actibus propriis dirigeretur per legem divinitus datam." Note that the Divine law is not necessary "that we may know what to do absolutely," but rather, "that we may know *without doubt*." This is an important distinction. To read that Divine law is necessary that we know the natural law is to read something into the text which is not there.

30. *ST* I-II, q. 91, a. 4, co.

31. *ST* I-II, q. 91, a. 4, co.: "Iudicium autem hominis esse non potest de interioribus motibus, qui latent, sed solum de exterioribus actibus, qui apparent."

32. *ST* I-II, q. 96, a. 2, co.

33. *ST* I-II, q. 91, a. 4, co.: "Ut ergo nullum malum improhibitum et impunitum remaneat, necessarium fuit supervenire legem divinam, per quam omnia peccata prohibentur."

34. *ST* I-II, q. 99, a. 3, ad 2: "[P]raecepta legis naturae communia sunt, et indigent determinatione. Determinatur autem et per legem humanam, et per legem divinam."

35. *ST* I-II, q. 98, a.1, co.

36. *ST* I-II, q. 100, a. 10, ad 3: "[O]bservare omnia praecepta legis homo non potest, nisi implead praeceptum caritatis...Et ideo impossibile est quod... hominem implore legem sine gratia."

37. *ST* I-II, q. 108, a.1, co.

38. *ST* I-II, q. 107, a. 1, ad 2.

39. *ST* II-II, q. 85, a. 1, s.c.

40. *Ibid.*

A NATURAL LAW CRITIQUE OF MILL'S ARGUMENT FOR JUSTICE

James Jacobs

In the final chapter of his *Utilitarianism,* John Stuart Mill constructs an argument to define justice in terms of general utility. Mill recognizes that offering such an argument is necessary, for it is not apparent how the utilitarian principle of maximizing the greatest happiness can provide for exceptionless moral norms, since the consequentialist position appears to undermine any attempt to establish rights that must always be respected *regardless of consequences*. Therefore, Mill attempts to show that utilitarianism can account for such rights by defining them with reference to man's desire for pleasure, to wit, his need for a feeling of security with respect to the basic goods of life. In this paper, I will examine Mill's argument in order to make two points. First, I will criticize what I take to be a very problematic mode of argumentation employed by Mill: he defines justice as a negation of injustice. While this enables Mill to define justice in terms of maximal pleasure, it also makes it impossible for his notion of justice to succeed in fulfilling its most basic criterion, a feeling of security in the possession of these rights. Second, by reference to the principles of natural law, I will elucidate the fundamental problem with Mill's approach. Natural law theory understands that what man can do is divided between two analogical uses of potentiality. While the precepts of the natural law are grounded in real potency based on the natural dynamism of being, Mill bases possibility on the desires that can be predicated of man, even those desires deficient of the fullness of being. This lack of specificity and objectivity means that Mill's theory can never establish any precept with the certitude necessary to provide people with the security he seeks to establish. While my argument is not intended be a global critique of utilitarianism as such, I hope to show how the principles of natural law help to illuminate a radical dilemma for any philosophy which attempts to define morality without reference to the objective dynamism of human nature, for it is this dynamism that is the necessary rule for adjudicating between subjective interests and objective needs and so is the only reliable foundation for determining what is truly owed to people.

MILL'S PROBLEMATIC PREMISE

In the Introduction to *Utilitarianism*, Mill states that one of his main motivations for writing the book is to correct what he takes to be common misunderstandings of utilitarian doctrine that had impeded its reception and prevented people from accepting the truth of its doctrine.[1] One of the more conspicuous difficulties he confronts is to render an account of justice within the context of utilitarian theory. The problem is that utilitarianism is committed to defining the good in terms of expedient consequences—that act is good which brings about the greatest amount of pleasure of the greatest number of people[2]—while the idea of justice implies an absolute—a principle that ought to be observed regardless of the consequences. Thus, as Ivan Karamazov might observe, to torture a child is always wrong, even if it were to guarantee the eternal happiness of the rest of mankind,[3] yet a utilitarian calculus would seem to warrant such an act. Indeed, even though Bentham had notoriously rejected the idea of rights as "nonsense upon stilts," because the idea of rights had become fundamental to modern discourse about justice, Mill must show that utilitarianism can accommodate our intuitions about objective rights as manifested in exceptionless rules of justice that can never be violated, regardless of consequences. Mill acknowledges the need for the obligatory nature of justice when he concludes his discussion with the claim that "justice is a name for certain classes of moral rules which concern the essentials of human well-being more nearly, and are therefore of more absolute obligation, than any other rules for the guidance of life."[4] The critical element here is the vague notion of the "essentials of human well-being," for this allows Mill to define justice in terms of utility. This is made clear in an alternate definition he offers a few pages later: "Justice is a name for certain moral requirements, which, regarded collectively, stand higher in the scale of social utility, and are therefore of more paramount obligation."[5] These definitions fit the utilitarian criteria because they are consequentialist; but note the vagueness that makes them open to revision in light of more satisfying consequences. This resolution brings together both obligation and consequentialism, and determines how he approaches the argument as a whole.

Before turning to Mill's account of the nature of justice,[6] let me make one clarification about how I understand that notion. While it is true that justice can be seen as an individual virtue, or habit, for that habit to be truly normative, it must in turn point to some transcendent absolute, a moral order which acts as the standard for moral action. The reason for this is brought out in Aquinas' appropriation of the Aristotelian tradition. While Aquinas follows Aristotle very closely in the idea of justice as a virtue,[7] he adds greater depth by framing justice as an abstract absolute standard that provides a foundation for the virtue.[8] The principle reason for this difference is that where Aristotle sees practical reason as applicable solely to contingent truths,[9] Aquinas understands that practical reason, as an extension of speculative reason, grasps universal principles of acting, that is, absolute laws.[10] Furthermore, Aquinas identifies these universal principles with the precepts of the Decalogue,[11] which are nothing but the immediate conclusions from the self-evident principles of the natural law.[12] But because the natural law is the participation of rational creatures in the eternal law (the providential order of creation),[13] it can be seen that the precepts of justice are embedded in the eternal law, a transcendent objective standard to which all men have recourse.[14] This transcendent standard both orders the universe and, through the natural law, gives man substantive moral principles about the nature of justice to be pursued. These universal precepts of the natural law, then, are seen to be the foundation for the virtue, which is the habit of acting in accord with this providential order of the universe.[15] Now, however one constitutes this transcendent standard, it is nevertheless the case that while justice can always be considered an habitual disposition, that disposition must have reference to some absolute standard. Thus, when I later refer to Mill's notion of justice as "privative," it is with respect to the absolute standard of justice.

Mill begins his discussion by acknowledging that a sense of justice as an absolute norm is natural for most men, and one so strong that it appears to have been given by some special revelation. He then notes that despite this feeling of a transcendent and objective origin for justice, his aim is to show that it is really only a special application of general utility. However, he immediately posits what I take to be the key problematic premise for his argument: "To throw light upon this question, it is necessary to attempt to ascertain what is the distinguishing character of justice, *or of injustice*; what is the quality, or whether there is any quality, attributed in common to all modes of conduct designated as unjust (for *justice, like many other moral attributes, is best defined by its opposite*)."[16] Note the crucial shift in Mill's argument: he is not establishing the nature of justice; on the contrary, he is establishing the nature of *injustice* and he assumes that justice is merely its negation.[17] Mill then proceeds to discern a common element characteristic of injustice to show that is explicable in terms of utility. As I will argue, he can only explain justice in terms of utilitarian criteria by starting with injustice, which leaves his notion of justice both vague and underspecified, and so open to revision; this vagueness, in turn, will undermine his theory as a whole.

Before continuing with Mill's argument, we need to elaborate on why Mill's shift from arguing about justice to arguing about injustice is in fact problematic. It is perfectly true that we define negations relative to some absolute;[18] yet it is crucially important which of the two is understood to be the term representing positive content, a term which signifies absolutely as bearing the intelligibility characteristic of the real, while the other term signifies only relatively as a parasitic negation of that positive intelligible content. Aristotle, developing a line of thought going back to Pythagoras, argues for the importance of the notion of contrariety for metaphysics: "Again, in the list of contraries one of the two columns is privative, and all contraries are reducible to being and non-being, and to unity and plurality, as for instance rest belongs to unity and movement to plurality.... It is obvious then from these considerations too that it belongs to one science to examine being *qua* being. For all things are either contraries or composed of contraries."[19] Thus, contraries all reduce to being or its negation, and everything else must be able to be discussed in terms of these principles. This provides the critical clue about discerning the priority between contraries. For, as a principle articulated by Aquinas notes, a thing is knowable inasmuch as it is in act.[20] That is, things are knowable inasmuch as they are actively present in the world, an active presence by which the entity reveals its nature to other beings.[21] It is this presence that is intelligible, since we grasp reality in terms of this universal truth and define privations parasitically in terms of a lack of that actively present intelligibility. Thus, being (and unity, truth, goodness, beauty) has priority over non-being (and plurality, falsity, evil, ugliness),[22] because being is that which is directly knowable in the nature of experience itself.

To illustrate this, consider how discovery is made: before any concept of an entity is formed, we first discover some activity, we are made aware of something happening in the field of consciousness; if that activity, an active presence, is inexplicable in terms of already known agents, then we posit the existence of a new substantial entity whose activity is revealing its presence to the environment. This invites more study, through which we (eventually, it is hoped) come to isolate and discern the essence of the entity. It is from this experience of activity that entities are then named, but an incompletely understood essence leaves itself open to revision once further experience clarifies the nature of the thing's interaction with its environment. Indeed, in 2011, the Nobel Prize in Physics was awarded to researchers for the discovery of "dark energy," an as-yet mysterious phenomenon, yet which is made known by means of its active presence in the universe. Crucially, despite their ignorance of what precisely dark energy is, the physicists clearly assert its reality as a scientific truth.²³ Thus, the correlation of intelligibility and being underlies the pole to which we give precedence; it is not an arbitrary presumption, but rather one which is based on the fact that man, in seeking understanding, has to grasp that for which evidence is immediately present.²⁴ That which is present is that which is actual, and the negation of actuality is non-being, which is nothing (literally), whose utter lack of intelligibility—it is impossible to even conceive of nothing—cannot be grasped except by way of privation from being.

This is pertinent for our argument since, as contraries, we must be able to discern whether justice or injustice has priority in terms of being. More typically, a philosopher would see justice as the pole of intelligible reality, and injustice as the privation to it. Thus, inasmuch as justice is taken to be a species of good, and good is convertible with being, it is natural to assume that justice has intelligible priority. So, for example, in defining evil as a privative reality, Aquinas affirms, "One opposite is known through the other, as darkness is known through light. Hence also what evil is must be known from the nature of good."²⁵ That this relation of positive intelligible content is tied to the more fundamental idea of the real is made clear in Aquinas' consideration of the ways in which things are predicated of the verb "to be":

> We should notice, therefore, that the word "being," taken without qualifiers, has two uses.... (1) In one way, it is used apropos of what is divided into the ten genera; (2) in another way, it is used to signify the truth of propositions. The difference between the two is that in the second way everything about which we can form an affirmative proposition can be called a being, even though it posits nothing in reality. It is in this way that privations and negations are called beings; for we say that affirmation is opposed to negation, and that blindness is in the eye. In the first way, however, only what posits something in reality can be called a being.²⁶

Although we talk about negations as if they were intelligible realities in themselves, that illusion is easily overcome by grasping the analogical nature of being. Donut holes are said to exist only insofar they are privations of the reality that is knowable *per se*. Since it is the pole of intelligible reality that must have precedence, we can see that the privative pole—representing a negation of the real intelligibility, and so unthinkable in itself—is parasitic on the real;[27] that is, only when we grasp the intelligible content of the real can we understand the negation, for it is precisely insofar as the negation lacks the wholeness of that intelligibility that we are aware of it at all.

This has two important implications for my argument. First, while the negation can be fully grasped only in light of the real, it is nevertheless also true that the intuition of privation can manifest itself in emotive terms. Indeed, privations which of their nature escape understanding due to their lack of intelligible being are nonetheless often viscerally grasped due to the fact of their privativeness. For example, an intelligible explanation of a monstrous evil like a terrorist attack can elude even the most articulate person, yet all recognize the fact of the evil; an ugly event instills disgust, even for those who lack an aesthetic philosophy. This is because man has a natural tendency to the fullness of being, and the frustration of that ontological exigence is immediately grasped emotively as a natural reaction to impediments to flourishing. Thus, that one takes offense at injustice is not surprising, for it is the nature of man to respond to privations emotionally as well as (indeed, prior to) intellectually. Thus, when Mill finds a sense of offense common to injustice, it cannot be taken to be indicative of the essence of *justice*. Second, this point is exacerbated when one considers a complex reality might possess multiple notes of intelligibility, so the privation of any one of these notes represents a lack of the complete intelligible whole. But this means that "reverse engineering" an intelligible reality is largely impossible, for if one defines the negation merely by noting one privation, it in no way leads to the recognition of all the other intelligible realities that ought to be present.

I have emphasized this point to highlight the novelty of Mill's argument in which he takes the counter-intuitive position: we can best understand justice by defining injustice. By means of this maneuver, he can define justice in terms of an obligation to avoid the unpleasantness of injustice, yet this also allows him to accommodate the consequentialist revisions of justice since what is considered unpleasant is not necessarily constant. But, by avoiding the positive reality of justice, he leaves its precepts vague and underspecified, and therefore justice as conceived by Mill can never provide the security he believes is necessary to make its obligations absolute.

MILL'S ARGUMENT TO DEFINE JUSTICE

Let us therefore return to Mill's argument to demonstrate how his assumption of the primacy of injustice leads his argument astray. Mill begins by acknowledging that there is a vast array of rather different phenomena which men are wont to classify as just or unjust. It is interesting to note, though, that in the main instances which follow, Mill gives precedence to injustice: "It is mostly considered unjust to deprive anyone of his personal liberty, his property, or any other thing which belongs to him by law," a truth yielding a notion of legal rights;[28] yet, acknowledging the existence of unjust laws, he admits of a higher criterion, and so concludes "a second case of injustice consists in taking or withholding from any person that to which he has a moral right." He follows this with quick assertions that it is unjust to obtain a good or suffer an evil one does not deserve, to break faith or disappoint expectations, or to be partial or biased.[29] Mill then asserts that since "it is a matter of some difficulty to seize the mental link which holds [these examples of injustice] together," we ought to consider the etymology for some direction in finding the "moral sentiment adhering to the term" on which the understanding of injustice depends.[30]

The etymology of the term shows that in many languages the root is tied to legal ordinances.[31] While admitting that etymology is a very inexact sort of evidence, Mill does argue that it can reveal the "primitive element in the formation of the notion of justice" as conformity to law. He concludes from this that injustice fundamentally means "the sentiment...attached, not to all violations of the law [since some laws are unjust], but only to violations of such laws as *ought* to exist."[32] Thus, the existence of a particular law is irrelevant to the idea of injustice, since there are many areas of life that are impossible, or at least impractical, to regulate by law, which nevertheless instill in us a sentiment that people ought to behave a certain way. Therefore, he arrives at the essential criterion for discerning injustice: a desire to punish someone for violating an apparent obligation or duty (that for which there ought to be a law). Thus, he concludes, "the idea of penal sanction, which is the essence of law, enters not only into the conception of injustice, but into that of any kind of wrong. We do not call anything wrong unless we mean to imply that a person ought to be punished in some way or other for doing it—if not by law, by the opinion of his fellow creatures; if not by opinion, by the reproaches of his own conscience."[33]

Note that throughout this argument, Mill has given priority to injustice, and so arrives at its essence in terms of deserving of punishment; yet he cannot describe *what* is deserving of punishment, nor *why* it is so deserving. Had he started with justice, he would have been required to answer both of these. Mill's argument does enable him to go on to provide an interpretation of justice and rights in terms of utilitarian principles, but at the cost of not grounding that justice on positively definable limits. This is pertinent, for his next step is to argue that the corollary to the idea of "ought to be punished" is that duty is what is exacted from another on pain of punishment.[34] Thus, while we acknowledge that there are many things that one might disapprove of in another, only very few of these disapprobations incite in us the desire to punish; those actions that incite this strong resentment are seen to be tied to a duty,[35] which in turn generates absolute moral rules everyone ought to respect. Mill defines justice, then, in terms of these absolute claims: "Justice implies something which it is not generally only right to do, and wrong not to do, but which some individual person can claim from us as his moral right."[36] Since injustice is based on a desire for punishment, the negation defining justice is simply the claim made upon others not to suffer such violations.

Thus, injustice involves a wrong, plus some individual who has been wronged. What, though, is the source this sense of duty to punish this? If the feeling arises out of a prior idea of justice, then it is not part of utilitarianism; but if it arises out of sentiment, then the utilitarian theory can be defended. Mill asserts that the essential desire to punish the offender is comprised of two perfectly natural instincts: "the impulse of self-defense and the feeling of sympathy."[37] The first impulse defending self-interest is common to all animals, and the second impulse is unique to man only insofar as his rational nature enlarges his sympathy beyond his direct offspring to include all members of the human race. Thus, it is this sympathy that is the foundation for our recognition of the common interest, whence arises our sense of duty: it incites man to seek vengeance against anyone who threatens any community interest as if it were a threat to one's own. Mill puts forth his conclusion this way: "The sentiment of justice appears to me to be, the animal desire to repel or retaliate a hurt or damage to oneself or to those with whom one sympathizes, widened so as to include all persons by the human capacity of enlarged sympathy and the human conception of intelligent self-interest. From the latter elements, the feeling derives its morality; from the former, its peculiar impressiveness, and energy of self-assertion."[38] This definition is clearly within the compass of utilitarian criteria, for it is based on the desire for pleasure and to avoid pain; yet it is moral because the pleasure and avoidance of pain must be vouchsafed for the whole community because of the sympathy one feels.

Having shown how justice can be defined in terms of utility, Mill then defines *right* accordingly: "When we call anything a person's right, we mean that he has a valid claim on society to protect him in the possession of it, either by the force of law or by that of education and opinion."[39] That is, a right is any claim of offense that engenders enough public sympathy so that others will defend it.

This justification of rights hinges on "general utility," for there is a common interest in "security, to everyone's feelings the most vital of all interests."[40] So, with respect to the most fundamental goods, man needs a sense of abiding security; communal sympathy would guarantee that everyone would similarly desire protection of these most basic of goods under any circumstances, thus securing the peace of mind without which happiness could never be achieved. What this concretely implies for Mill is that those rules preventing harm are vital for inculcating peace and common flourishing. Their ultimate foundation is the desire for pleasure and avoidance of pain, which acts as "the same powerful motives which command the observance of these primary moralities [and also] enjoin the punishment of those who violate them."[41] Indeed, it is the expectation that others will defend me that is one of the strongest feelings and guarantors of common sympathy. This equal claim of everyone to basic elements of pleasure is for Mill both the essence of utilitarianism and the ground of his understanding of justice.

In short, for Mill, we enforce rights to protect a feeling of security, the most significant kind of utility; thus justice is the most important application of utility:

> While I dispute the pretensions of any theory which sets up an imaginary standard of justice not grounded on utility, I account the justice which is grounded on utility to be the chief part, and incomparably the most sacred and binding part, of all morality. Justice is a name for certain classes of moral rules, which concern the essentials of human well-being more nearly, and are therefore of more absolute obligation, than any other rules for the guidance of life; and the notion which we have found to be of the essence of the idea of justice, that of a right residing in an individual implies and testifies to this more binding obligation.[42]

Mill's argument has produced a theory of justice in which utility is clearly prior to justice; justice is defined not as an abstract absolute in itself, but on the basis of maximally good consequences (the maximization of pleasure of being secure in one's rights). He sees this lack of metaphysical certainty as further proof for his theory, for if rights were based on some positive intelligible reality, then they would be more clearly enumerable and universally grasped. Indeed, for Mill it is the radically divergent ideas of what constitutes a right that makes the principle of social utility the only reasonable basis for deciding which claims deserve respect.

On the other hand, this also points to the ultimate weakness in his argument. Because he defines rights in terms of his consequentialist theory, Mill recognizes that claims to rights are in fact variable and somewhat obscure; indeed, even his definition of justice cited earlier makes room for this: "Justice is a name for certain moral requirements, which, regarded collectively, stand higher in the scale of social utility, and are therefore of more paramount obligation, than any others; *though particular cases may occur in which some other social duty is so important, as to overrule any one of the general maxims of justice.*"[43] By subordinating rights to utility, Mill robs people of any security they might have been supposed to have had; by subjecting principle to consequentialist criterion, he erodes the stability of the principle.[44] Thus, he undermines his own criteria, for if people cannot feel secure that their rights will not be overridden, then there is no justification for his notion of right.[45]

This is the inevitable consequence of starting off by defining injustice, for this leaves the precepts of justice vague and underspecified. As mentioned earlier, to start one's investigation by searching for the privation of justice allows one to find at least one quality characteristic of justice. However, it is unlikely that that approach would discover the fullness of being characteristic of justice; yet it is this that would establish truly invariable principles that would provide the security Mill seeks. From pointing out the obvious fact that injustice is tied to a sense of offense and a sentiment of vengeance, Mill is simply stating a tautological fact, for a wrong is privative. But it is illegitimate to define justice wholly in terms of sympathetic concern for that offense. This is why starting with injustice obscures the true, complex nature of justice: from the fact of darkness, no one could guess the splendor of light; from the inertness of inorganic matter, no one could imagine the exuberance of life. Thus, from the sense of being wronged, it is unlikely that one would really grasp the true nature of justice in its fullness.[46] While his refusal to define concretely the precepts of justice makes more reasonable his claim that the principles are subject to revision, it also severely saps those principles of any security they may offer people. For as society changes, what had been seen as sacred is sacrificed to expediency. However, this means that there are no *rights*, for ephemeral rights are not rights at all. For example, while Mill argues that everyone would always respect the idea that people ought not be directly harmed,[47] who counts as a person and what constitutes harm are underspecified and subject to the utilitarian calculation with respect to desirable consequences. Accordingly, for many today abortion and euthanasia are now proclaimed to harm no one, and depriving a child of biological parents and seizing the property of the wealthy are not seen to constitute harm.

A CRITIQUE BASED ON THE ANALOGICAL NATURE OF BEING

In this final section of the paper, I will use the principles of the natural law to demonstrate why Mill's argument—giving precedence to injustice, and then defining justice with reference to a feeling of security—was destined to failure. The problem is that consequentialism defines rights in terms of interests to be achieved; injustice is any violation of those *interests*, and so a right exists when each individual can be secure that his interests will be defended. This emphasis on interests, however, plays upon a univocal flattening of the notion of potency as that which can be achieved. By attending to the natural law's distinction among senses of potentiality, we can see how Mill's understanding of injustice is based on a notion of potency that includes defect, and thus can never yield specific and invariably recognized rights. Natural law, on the other hand, defines potency in terms of the fullness of being which indicates, not subjective interests, but the actual ontological needs by which stable and unchanging rights can truly be derived.[48]

The analogical understanding of being is made necessary when one considers that while everything must be defined by reference to being (since otherwise it would be non-being, that is, nothing), it is nevertheless clear that things can be said to be in different ways.[49] We have already seen how Aquinas uses the analogy of being to distinguish real being and mind-dependent being, but he broadens its application by outlining four primary modes of being: substance, accident, potential, and negation or privation.[50] The primary mode of being is substance because substance is that which exists independently; the other modes are dependent on substance, but with decreasing embodiments of what it means to be actual. Thus, accidents are actual, but are dependent modes of being parasitic on substance; potency is not now actual but is what could be, although that potency to be is circumscribed and defined by the substance as now constituted; and negation and privation are non-being, but, as argued above, because absolute non-being is inconceivable, it is a non-being parasitic on substantial being. Thus, "Since corruption terminates in privation just as generations terminates in form, the very privations of substantial forms are fittingly called beings."[51] Because privations and negations can be the subject of true predications, they can be said to have being in a mind-dependent fashion.

The analogical nature of being is such that only substances have being in the primary sense and with complete intelligibility, while the dependent modes of being have intelligibility only with reference to these substances: "The second type of division is that which is common by analogy: namely, that which is predicated of one of the things to which it is common according to its complete intelligibility, and of the other according to an imperfect intelligibility and with some qualification (*secundum quid*). Thus, being is divided into substance and accidents, and into being in act and being in potency."[52] What I would argue is that there is a real difference between the real potentiality as circumscribed and defined by the substance, and the merely logical possibility associated with that which can be predicated of the substance in some way.[53] And it is this difference that will demonstrate why Mill's giving primacy to injustice as a violation of interest cannot generate stable principles of justice.

To understand this liability of Mill's argument, we must grasp the profoundly teleological nature of natural law, for a nature is defined not by reference to an inert essence but by its dynamic tendencies to the fullness of its being.[54] This dynamism is implicit in the common Latin denomination for quiddity, *quod quid erat esse*, the-what-it-was-to-be of the substance, which clearly brings out the end-directedness that is constitutive of every essence.[55] Since every substance is a composition of a quiddity with the *act* of existence,[56] once actualized (in first act) there is a dynamism (to second act) that is not just appropriate to, but definitive of, that substance's nature. This point is most clearly articulated in Aquinas' repeated claim that everything exists for the sake of its perfective operation: "Indeed, all things created would seem, in a way, to be purposeless, if they lacked an operation proper to them; since the purpose of everything is its operation. For the less perfect is always for the sake of the more perfect: and consequently as the matter is for the sake of the form, so the form which is the first act, is for the sake of its operation, which is the second act; and thus operation is the end of the creature."[57] That this defining dynamism determines the specific content of justice is made clear in Aquinas' argument that "according to the order of natural inclinations is the order of the precepts of the natural law."[58]

This understanding of essence in terms of the fullness of being has important implications for our understanding of man's potency to act. Because the entity is ordered to that fullness, potentiality most properly refers to those ends toward which an essence is ordered. That is, the real potentiality of human nature is embodied by those activities perfective of its natural dynamisms. There is an analogical use of potential, though, that refers to all those things that *can* be done by human agency, although inasmuch as they do not embody the perfection of man's natural dynamism, they must be seen as being inherently defective or privative.

The critical point here is that Aquinas' presentation of the analogy of being enables us to distinguish on principle the difference between what man ought to do in terms of having real ontological potency as evidenced by his essential dynamism, and what man can do in terms of a logical possibility of being an interest of a human agent. Only the former entails the fullness of being.[59] In fact, we can say that the latter, since it includes privation, is activity only in an equivocal sense, since act ought to perfect the being. While the following argument is about transitive causality, the same principle can be readily applied to the immanent causality of operations[60].

> Since every agent acts inasmuch as it is actual and consequently produces its like, the form of the thing produced must in some manner be in the agent: in different ways, however. When the effect is proportionate to the power of the agent, this form must be of the same kind in the maker and the thing made.... When, however, the effect is improportionate to the power of the cause, the form is not of the same kind in both maker and thing made, but is in the agent in a more eminent way.[61]

This is why human acts can be ontologically good, inasmuch as they possess existence at all, yet morally privative as not embodying the fullness of being.[62] Acting on interests, as opposed to ontological needs, is to fail to attain the fullness of human being, and so is inherently defective in character.

This illuminates the problem with Mill's argument. Inasmuch as utilitarianism is interested in maximizing the interests of people—not the ontological needs, but the subjective preferences for pleasure—those interests are predicated of man as something that he *can do* or something that *might be* desired. Yet, since they are not defined with respect to man's real potency, they belong more to the realm of mind-dependent beings, as privations contrary to natural fulfillment, than the real potency indicative of the essence. They are logical possibilities of preference, not ontological potentialities. Thus, anything can be desired, and there is no reference to reality by which to delimit those preferences; if nature is not the norm, then man's interests become the norm.⁶³ This is why Mill starts with injustice, for he has to allow for a consequentialist revisionism which can only be accomplished if he ignores the real potentiality associated with specific precepts of justice. Yet, because of the indefiniteness of what can be predicated of man's desire, the notion of justice that emerges cannot have the stability or certitude required to ground a meaningful sense of invariable rights.⁶⁴ This is easily contrasted with the fullness of being as reflected in the natural law which allows for the specific enumeration of unchanging rights.

An illustration of what happens when this analogical sense of potential is ignored, and preference is given to mind-dependent "interests" instead of the objective needs associated with real potency, can be seen in the unintended evolution of the Fourteenth Amendment to the U.S. Constitution. The past few decades have witnessed a shift from reading this amendment in terms of justice as protecting rights constitutive of human dignity, to seeing justice as defending claims based on any thinkable interest.⁶⁵ This amendment says that no person shall be denied the equal protection of the law. Originally drafted in the wake of Emancipation, the amendment was intended to guarantee the political freedom and human dignity of former slaves. This principle of non-discrimination seems to embody the essence of justice as a necessary prerequisite for common human flourishing. However, as rights have become identified with ill-defined interests, courts have been led to read this principle of non-discrimination as preventing the government from taking any substantive moral position whatsoever, lest that moral position offend the sentiments of some dissident group.⁶⁶ A consequence of this insistence on substantive neutrality with respect to moral issues is, for example, that the mere desire for some benefit (contraception, abortion, homosexual marriage) must be given equal standing with the objective needs and virtues (religion, temperance, familial structure). While needs in terms of objective potentiality can be defined and enumerated, interests have no limit. But if jurisprudence is to protect interests, then no interest is truly protected, since it can be infringed upon in light of ever evolving exigencies which necessarily involves conflicts between interests.[67] Thus, to be secure in the right to abortion or free contraception is seen to be equal to the right to religious freedom. The only way to arbitrate this is by sheer expediency, and so some find themselves not as secure in their rights as they had supposed.

This argument in itself may not persuade those who reject the analogy of being, including followers of Mill. Yet it does illustrate how the natural law's commitment to the real—not just in act, but real potency as opposed to mere logical possibility—can ground rights with greater security than could be had otherwise. In this way, natural law continues to provide chastening guidance for our age, an age which Allan Bloom has described as one in which "there are no ends, only possibilities."[68] But, the more we are bewitched by this sense of possibility, the more we lose our sense of end, the less secure our rights become.

NOTES

1. In his in his introductory "General Remarks," Mill asserts "the very imperfect notion ordinarily formed of [utilitarianism's] meaning is the chief obstacle which impedes its reception, and that, could it be cleared even from only the grosser misconceptions, the question would be greatly simplified and a large proportion of its difficulties removed" (John Stuart Mill, *Utilitarianism*, ed. by George Sher, 2nd Edition (Indianapolis: Hackett, 2001), 5).

2. See *Utilitarianism*, 7: "The creed which accepts as the foundation of morals 'utility' or the Greatest Happiness Principle holds that actions are right in proportion as they tend to promote happiness; wrong as they tend to produce the reverse of happiness. By happiness is intended pleasure and the absence of pain; by unhappiness, pain, and the privation of pleasure."

It should be noted that while Mill follows Bentham very closely in equating happiness with pleasure, he nonetheless attempts to refine that notion so that pleasure is less the crude sensationalism of Bentham and more like Aristotle's idea of *eudaimonia* (see the Chapter II, 7-15). Addressing the objection that that focus on pleasure and pain is a "doctrine worthy only on swine," Mill takes pains to show that utilitarianism considers not just the quantity of pleasure, but also the quality. Humans have a natural inclination to a different sort of pleasure, the pleasure of the intellect, and so because "human beings have faculties more elevated than the animal appetites...[they] do not regard anything as happiness which does not include their gratification." Thus, happiness is "not a life of rapture, but moments of such, in an existence made up of few and transitory pains, many and various pleasure, with a decided predominance of the active over the passive," which he identifies with the life of a "cultivated mind" which finds pleasure in science, and art, and poetry. This is both reminiscent of Aristotle's "living well and faring well" (*NE* I.4, 1095a19), as well as appealing to a common sense insight about the nature of man and the truly despairing nature of a life of hedonistic pleasure.

It must be said, however, that Mill's attempt to incorporate qualitatively higher pleasures into the criterion for utilitarianism largely fails, for two reasons. First, the argument by which the higher pleasures are discovered is circular. He begins by arguing, "Of two pleasures, if there be one to which all or almost all who have experienced both give a decided preference...that is the more desirable pleasure." However, faced with the obvious empirical fact that the large majority of people prefer (in our day) reality television and junk food to reading Shakespeare and listening to opera, Mill then argues that the "capacity for other nobler feelings is in most natures a very tender plant, easily killed," and so most men are no longer capable of appreciating the higher pleasures. Thus, in consulting the "only competent judges," we can discern which pleasures are of a higher quality. But to exclude the opinion of the majority of people in this judgments invalidates his original premise that the higher pleasure is the one that most people naturally choose.

The second reason why Mill's argument to establish the relevance of higher pleasures as a criterion for utilitarianism fails is because in order to establish it, he brings in another criterion, human dignity, which means he is implicitly rejecting the fact of pleasure as the principle upon which this theory stands. He argues that "dignity, which all human beings possess in one form or other...[in] proportion to the higher faculties" is essential to happiness, and no one would surrender that for mere physical pleasure: "It is better to be a human being dissatisfied than a pig satisfied; better to be Socrates dissatisfied than a fool satisfied." But this is to turn utilitarianism itself into a kind of natural law: if you assume there is a principle other than pleasure by which some pleasures are determined to be more truly human (i.e., dignified), then you simply are not making a utilitarian argument anymore. Indeed, even Mill's assumption that there are qualitatively different pleasures implies that he must introduce a principle other than pleasure itself as a criterion for moral judgment, since all pleasures, *qua* pleasure, are only quantitatively different. (This argument follows Alasdair MacIntyre, *A Short History of Ethics: A History of Moral Philosophy from the Homeric Age to the Twentieth Century* (New York: Touchstone, 1996), 235-236.) If one grants that happiness is not merely pleasure, one has already sided with Aristotle against the utilitarian principle.

3. See *Brothers Karamazov*, Pt. II, Bk. V, Ch. 4: "Rebellion."
4. *Utilitarianism*, 59.
5. *Utilitarianism*, 63.
6. This argument is contained in Chapter V of *Utilitarianism*, 42-64.
7. *ST* II-II.57-58.
8. I have developed this argument at greater length in "The Metaethical Inclusiveness of Natural Law Theory" in *Nova et Vetera* (English edition) 7.2 (Spring 2009): 361-388, especially at 382-386.
9. *Nicomachean Ethics* VI.1 (1139a5-15). This explains Aristotle's repeated insistence on the difficulty of the moral life; see, for example, *Nicomachean Ethics* II.9 (1109a24-29): "Hence also it is not easy task to be good.... [T]o do

this to the right person, to the right extent, at the right time, with the right motive, and in the right way, *that* is not for everyone, nor it is easy; wherefore goodness is both rare and laudable and noble." (Translation by W. D. Ross (Oxford: Oxford World's Classics, 1998)).

10. In other words, where Aristotle divides the intellect into the scientific and calculative, Aquinas says the intellect is unified. On Aquinas' rejection of Aristotle's division of the intellect, see *ST* I.79.11 and his *Commentary on Aristotle's "Nicomachean Ethics"* VI.1.1123; see also the discussion of this in Denis J.M. Bradley, *Aquinas on the Twofold Human Good: Reason and Human Happiness in Aquinas's Moral Science* (Washington, D.C.: Catholic University of America Press, 1997), esp. at 154: "Aquinas rescues Aristotelian *phronesis* from any ambiguous conjunction and perhaps subordination to desire and acquired habituation by anchoring prudential reasoning in a set of universal, immediate, primary principles that structure and direct practical reason, principles that, in turn, are said to participate in the divine mind itself."

11. *ST* II-II.122.1.

12. *ST* I-II.100.1 and 11.

13. *ST* I-II.91.2: "Now among all others, the rational creature is subject to Divine providence in the most excellent way, in so far as it partakes of a share of providence, by being provident both for itself and for others. Wherefore it has a share of the Eternal Reason, whereby it has a natural inclination to its proper act and end: and this participation of the eternal law in the rational creature is called the natural law." All citations are taken from the translation by the Fathers of the English Dominican Province (New York: Benzinger, 1948; reprint, Allen, TX: Christian Classics, 1981).

14. *ST* I-II.93.3 and 6. This revision of Aristotle is also reflected in Aquinas' replacement of the centrality of the polis in Aristotelian ethics to a focus on all of creation. A good analysis of the shortcomings Aquinas finds in Aristotle's moral theory is in Mary M. Keys, *Aquinas, Aristotle, and the Promise of the Common Good* (Cambridge: Cambridge University Press, 2006), 102-109 and 124.

15. *ST* I-II.94.3: "To the natural law belongs everything to which a man is inclined according to his nature. Now each thing is inclined naturally to an operation that is suitable to it according to its form: thus fire is inclined to give heat. Wherefore, since the rational soul is the proper form of man, there is in every man a natural inclination to act according to reason: and this is to act according to virtue. Consequently, considered thus, all acts of virtue are prescribed by the natural law: since each one's reason naturally dictates to him to act virtuously." This is also reflected in the fact that in ST II-II.57, Aquinas discusses the objective nature of the "right" (*jus)* prior to introducing his discussion of the virtue of justice.

16. *Utilitarianism*, 43; emphasis mine.

17. That Mill introduces this crucial inversion in a parenthetical statement should not distract us from noting its eccentricity, for it is natural that one attempt rhetorically to obscure problematic steps in an argument.

18. As Aristotle points out, knowledge of contraries is the same; see *Topics* I.14 (105b30-36).

19. See Aristotle, *Metaphysics* IV.2 (1004b27-30), translation by W.D. Ross in *The Basic Works of Aristotle*, ed. by Richard McKeon (New York: Random House, 1941). Aristotle examines the Pythagorean lineage in *Met.* I.5 (986a22-986b8). For the background to this discussion, see Joseph Owens, *The Doctrine of Being in the Aristotelian 'Metaphysics,'* 3rd edition (Toronto: Pontifical Institute of Medieval Studies, 1978), 275-9.

20. See, for example, *Summa Theologica* I.5.2: "Now the first thing conceived by the intellect is being; because everything is knowable only inasmuch as it is in actuality. Hence, being is the proper object of the intellect, and is primarily intelligible." See also *ST* I.87.1.

21. On this, see W. Norris Clarke, SJ, "Action as the Self-Revelation of Being: A Central Theme in the Thought of St. Aquinas" in *Explorations in Metaphysics: Being, God, Person* (Notre Dame, IN: University of Notre Dame Press, 1995), 45-64.

22. One will recognize that this list of primary intelligibles is the traditional list of the transcendental properties. Aquinas argues that transcendental properties are primary because they are self-evident to all, while the truth associated with any specific nature is self-evident in itself but not to all because the knowledge of any specific nature is contingent and so not given universally, whereas the transcendental properties are necessarily present in each and every experience of being; see *ST* I.2.1 and I-II.94.2.

23. Aquinas recognizes this type of argument when he makes a distinction between two sorts of proofs: one sort of argument, from effects to causes, is able to demonstrate that a cause exists, yet because the effects do not fully manifest the nature of the cause, we do not (yet) fully grasp the nature of the cause; on the other hand, if the effects fully manifest the essence of the cause, we can argue from cause to effect, an argument which explains the entirety of the effect in question; see *ST* I.2.2.

24. The self-contradictory nature of post-modern objections to this is noted in Alasdair MacIntyre, *Three Rival Versions of Moral Enquiry: Encyclopaedia, Genealogy, and Tradition* (Notre Dame, IN: University of Notre Dame Press, 1991), 196-215.

25. *ST* I.48.1.

26. *De Ente et Essentia*, c.1; translation from Joseph Bobik, *Aquinas on Being and Essence: A Translation and Interpretation* (Notre Dame, IN: University of Notre Dame Press, 1965), 21.

27. See *De Malo* 1.1; see also Brian Davies' Introduction to Richard Regan's translation, *On Evil* (Oxford: Oxford University Press, 2003).

28. *Utilitarianism*, 44.

29. *Utilitarianism*, 45.

30. *Utilitarianism*, 47.

31. He cites in particular the Latin *justum*, the Greek *dikaion*, the German *recht*, and the French *la justice*.

32. *Utilitarianism*, 47.

33. *Utilitarianism*, 48-49.

34. *Utilitarianism*, 49: "We call any conduct wrong…according as we think that the person ought to, or ought not, to be punished for it; and we say it would be right to do so and so…according as we would wish to see the person whom it concerns compelled…to act in that manner." Notice again the priority given to wrong over right.

35. Mill specifies that this is restricted solely to what have traditionally been called "perfect duties," which oblige everyone absolutely, as opposed to imperfect duties, which act more like counsels exhorting supererogatory acts (like beneficence or charity). Thus, only perfect duties can be said to generate correlative rights.

36. *Utilitarianism*, 50; compare this to his final definition(s), referenced at notes 4 and 5 above, concerning those essentials of human well-being required by social utility.

37. *Utilitarianism*, 51.
38. *Utilitarianism*, 53.
39. *Utilitarianism*, 53.
40. *Utilitarianism*, 54.
41. *Utilitarianism*, 60.
42. *Utilitarianism*, 59.
43. *Utilitarianism*, 63; emphasis mine.
44. Indeed, Mill himself is clear that the morality is infinitely plastic, and can be shaped to value anything whatsoever; see *Utilitarianism*, Chapter III, esp. 31: "Like the other acquired capacities above referred to, the moral faculty... [is] susceptible of being brought by cultivation to a high degree of development. Unhappily it is also susceptible, by a sufficient use of the external sanctions and of the force of early impressions, of being cultivated in almost any direction."
45. Similar critiques of utilitarian consequentialism are presented in John Finnis, *Natural Law and Natural Rights* (Oxford: Clarendon Press, 1980) and Henry B. Veatch, *Human Rights: Fact or Fancy* (Baton Rouge: Louisiana State University Press, 1985).

Another way of putting this is that by making the principles of justice subordinate to utility, Mill robs them of the *authority* necessary to provide people a sense of security as the fundamental principle of order in society (see Yves R. Simon, *A General Theory of Authority* (South Bend, IN: University of Notre Dame Press, 1980). The essential function of authority is not simply to punish violators, but to guide free people to a common good; insofar as Mill's defines justice in solely in terms of punishment for violations, his understanding of justice cannot specify in absolute terms the constitutive elements of that common good, so the precepts of justice can never the authoritative and persuasive in and of themselves.

46. That the reality of justice is complex can be illustrated with reference to the fact that even Aquinas' simple definition—to give to each what is his due—engenders a great variety of considerations, for by this we can be said to owe some things to God (*ST* II-II.81), some things to others (as outlined in precepts of the Decalogue in II-II.122), and even some things to oneself (insofar as we owe to ourselves the development of virtue in order to attain the human *telos* of happiness; see *ST* II-II.58.2). Moreover, what is owed to others must itself be distinguished (following the Decalogue) according to what is owed to one's parents and country, and then what is owed to another individual, first in terms of actions, and then in words, and finally in thoughts (see the *Collation on the Ten Commandments)*. These are all based on the real potency to fullness of being in the perfection of human nature.

47. *Utilitarianism*, 59-61. In articulating his famous "harm principle" in *On Liberty*, Mill suggests that that any individual's interests alone are the defining criteria of what constitutes harm, thereby reinforcing the contingent nature of any such judgment.

48. For an insightful analysis of the difference between these two modes of analogy, especially with respect to the issue of evil as a privative limitation of being, see Yves R. Simon, "On Order in Analogical Sets" *New Scholasticism* 34. 1 (1960): 1-42.

49. It is outside the scope of this paper to engage the convoluted debates concerning the various modes of analogy employed in Thomistic philosophy. However, for an interpretation that would show this to be an analogy of proper

proportionality based upon the diminishing qualifications of being from being its most fundamental sense, see Steven A. Long, *Analogia Entis: On the Analogy of Being, Metaphysics, and the Act of Faith* (Notre Dame, IN: University of Notre Dame Press, 2011).

50. I am following his analysis in *Commentary on Aristotle's Metaphysics* IV.1. 539-43.

51. *Comm. Met.* IV.1.539.

52. II Sent, d. 42, q. 1. a. 3, cited in George Klubertanz, SJ. *St. Thomas Aquinas on Analogy: A Textual Analysis and Systematic Synthesis* (Eugene, Oregon: Wipf and Stock, 2009), 35-36.

53. See *Comm. Met.* V.9.897.

54. This point is particularly well emphasized in the polemical context of John Wild, *Plato's Modern Enemies and the Theory of Natural Law* (Chicago: University of Chicago Press, 1953).

55. See *On Being and Essence*, c. 1; cf. *Comm. Met.* VII.2.1270. The Latin is a translation of the Aristotelian *to ti en einai*; for an analysis, see Owens, *The Doctrine of Being in the Aristotelian 'Metaphysics'*, 180-188.

56. See *On Being and Essence*, c. 4; cf. *ST* I.3.4.

57. *ST* I.105.5; cf. *Summa Contra Gentiles*, III.113.1: "Each thing appears to exist for the sake of its operation; indeed, operation is the ultimate perfection of a thing." Citations from the translation by Anton Pegis, James Anderson, and Vernon Bourke (Notre Dame, IN: University of Notre Dame Press, 1975).

58. *ST* I-II.94.2.

59. See *SCG* I.43.2: "The magnitude of [a substance's] power likewise is measured from the magnitude of its action or its works. Of these magnitudes one follows the other. For, from the fact that something is in [first] act it is active, and hence the mode of the magnitude of its power is according to the mode in which it is completed in its act."

60. See *Comm. Met.* IX.8.1865: "But when nothing else is produced in addition to the activity of the potency, the actuality then exists in the agent as its perfection and does not pass over into something external in order to perfect it; for example, the act of seeing is in the one seeing as his perfection, and the act of speculating is in the one speculating, and life is in the soul (if we understand by life vital activity)."

61. *De Potentia* 7.5; translation from *On the Power of God*, translated by the English Dominican Fathers (Westminster, MD: Newman Press, 1952).

62. *ST* I-II.18.1: "We must therefore say that every action has goodness, in so far as it has being; whereas it is lacking in goodness, in so far as it is lacking in something that is due to its fullness of being; and thus it is said to be evil."

63. As John Wild comments, "We must not confuse what is good with our own opinions and wishes. We are in no position to legislate what is really good and bad. This humanistic pride is a delusion of utilitarianism. It is nature that first legislates independent of all arbitrary human decree" (*Plato's Modern Enemies*, 147).

64. Robert George has argued that any instrumental notion of reason, in which principles are subordinated to desire, makes it impossible to defend human rights; see Robert George, *The Clash of Orthodoxies: Law, Religion, and Morality in Crisis* (Wilmington, DE: ISI Books, 2001), 3-21.

65. The text of section one reads: "All persons born or naturalized in the United States, and subject to the jurisdiction thereof, are citizens of the United States and of the State wherein they reside. No State shall make or enforce any law

which shall abridge the privileges or immunities of citizens of the United States; nor shall any State deprive any person of life, liberty, or property, without due process of law; nor deny to any person within its jurisdiction the equal protection of the laws."

66. See the discussion of this in Hadley Arkes, *Natural Rights and the Right to Choose* (Cambridge: Cambridge University Press, 2002), 26-33.

67. Thus, Robert George (*Clash of Orthodoxies*, 104) describes one scholar's defense of this change: "[Ronald] Dworkin maintains that government violates the basic right to equal concern and respect when it restricts liberty on the ground that one citizen's conception of what makes for or detracts from a valuable and morally worthy way of life is superior to another citizen's conception." Because there is no reference to real potential behind many interests, all claims must be treated equally; as George points out, Dworkin fails to recognize the real distinction between judging positions differently and treating the people who hold those positions unequally.

68. Quoted in Robert R. Reilly, *Making Gay Okay: How Rationalizing Homosexual Behavior is Changing Everything* (San Francisco: Ignatius Press, 2014), 28.

SPAEMANN'S CRITIQUE OF NUCLEAR ENERGY: A RENEWED NATURAL LAW FOR THE 20TH-21ST CENTURIES[1]

Gregory Canning

INTRODUCTION

In his recent book on the German philosopher Robert Spaemann, Holger Zaborowski indicates the importance of the role that natural law has for Spaemann in an age marked by the rejection of the limitations and guidance inherent in "what the human being is." Zaborowski writes: ". . . it is not too difficult to understand why Spaemann . . . attempts to recollect the concept of natural law, once again in a way that tries to revitalize a 'past knowledge' without overlooking the challenges of modern thinking and its emphasis on freedom."[2] These challenges he speaks of are not merely epistemological, in that they concern only the mode of thinking characteristic of modernity, but also relate to the goal toward which this thinking strives. If only the former were the case, then it would simply be a matter of returning to a pre-modern conception of natural law. This, Spaemann asserts, cannot be the case, for the simple reason that a technological drive spurs on the thinking of modernity, which seeks to dominate nature through dividing the human from it and placing the human over it.[3] Our freedom and power to make things previously unimagined places us in a novel situation, according to Spaemann; and this new situation calls upon further reflection concerning our ethical responsibilities toward other humans (both contemporary and future) as well as plant and animal life throughout the natural world.

The novel situation that Spaemann has in mind concerns the Western, industrialized world's relation to the rest of the world in our use of nuclear energy.[4] After the recent disaster at the Fukushima nuclear facility in Japan in March 2011, Spaemann wrote a foreword to a collection of his past essays and interviews on the "peaceful use" of nuclear energy. In that foreword, Spaemann notes that the first use of nuclear power was non-peaceful (and, in fact, tremendously violent)—the bombs dropped on Hiroshima and Nagasaki to end the Second World War. In his view, this destructive purpose was not "accidental" and shows that this power, even in its "peaceful" use, must not simply be limited and guided through the planning of "specific additional security measures that are supposed to reduce the likelihood of a catastrophe," but rather forbidden altogether.[5] His reasons for drawing this conclusion form the material of this article.

My purpose here is to show how Spaemann revitalizes the conception of natural law through his thoughtful analysis of the complex environmental issue of nuclear energy. Reading through his arguments concerning nuclear energy is useful for two reasons: 1) it provides a sense of coherence to Spaemann's work by drawing attention to a part of it that has often been neglected in the English-speaking world; and 2) it shows that a renewed sense of the natural law may find a welcome place in the twenty-first century with its many concerns and questions that are, by all accounts, novel. In order to achieve the purpose above I will divide the article into three sections and a conclusion. In the first section, I will point out the parallel that Spaemann sees in the arguments for the non-peaceful and peaceful uses of nuclear power. This parallel sets the stage for his ethical argument against the peaceful use of nuclear power based on both the side-effects of action and the consequences for future generations. I will outline the connection between these two points of his argument in the second section. Next, in the third section, I show how his overall argument draws on the resources of a renewed conception of both human nature and nature in general, which raises again the possibility of a natural law for the atomic age. In the conclusion, I will highlight Spaemann's expansion of natural law to include the natural world itself as a matter of human responsibility and explain in what way he views such an expansion as necessary. Though this reconceptualization of natural law deviates from the

Aristotelian/Thomist conception, it reflects our deep contemporary concern for humanity's relationship to the environment.

THE "NO ALTERNATIVE" ARGUMENT

In the "Foreword" to his collected essays, op-ed pieces, and interviews on nuclear energy, Spaemann draws the reader's attention to the similarity between the argument of the proponents of the use of nuclear energy in the contemporary context and that of the supporters of nuclear armament in the 1950s and 1960s: "Even then we heard the argument there is *no alternative*.[6] Without this weapon [the atom bomb] the West supposedly would be defenseless against the Soviet—as yet still non-nuclear—threat if one had not already considered the alternative of higher defense spending and greater military might."[7] At this point, the Americans had a monopoly on the production of nuclear weapons for use against the Soviet Union in case of a breach of the agreements after World War II. The solution that the Americans presented for the defense of the West against the Soviet threat was the armament of their allies in Western Europe, which included West Germany. Spaemann contested the arguments that were presented by his German contemporaries for nuclear armament in his two essays "On the Philosophical-Theological Discussion about the Atom Bomb" (1960) and "The Destruction of Natural Right Theory of War: A Response to P. Gustav Gundlach, S.J." (1960).[8] In both essays, Spaemann draws attention to the fact that the original teaching of just war theory could no longer be sustained *unaltered* with the advent of nuclear weapons.

Even later, in the 1980s, in his letter to the author, Nobel-laureate and noted pacifist Heinrich Böll (September 12, 1984), Spaemann reiterated that it was not the question of a "radical peace movement" on the part of the West that would lead to the disarmament of the Soviet threat; rather, his concern from the beginning was that these weapons existed in the first place: "Here it was no longer the question of a 'yes' or 'no' to nuclear armament. This armament had indeed taken place long ago—rather it was the question of reducing the risk of war."[9] The fact the Americans had these weapons even if the Soviets did not (or were unable to keep pace with the Americans in terms of producing more and more nuclear weapons) was, nevertheless, unsettling. At that time, Spaemann agreed with the point made by the Russian physicist-turned-activist, Andrei Sakharov, that "only the contractually secured nuclear disarmament on both sides is a responsible perspective."[10] The "no alternative" argument that had been presented in the 50s and 60s and up through the 80s could not be maintained without the recognition that armament met a conditional necessity at the time—but nuclear armament in itself was not "without alternative."

More recently this argument has been set to the task of defending the "peaceful" use of nuclear energy now that the Cold War is over. According to Spaemann, the defenders of the use of nuclear power make the argument that there is "no alternative[11] to this technology at the moment" and thus it constitutes a kind of "bridge-technology"[12] to fill the gap until better alternatives are discovered.[13] (These alternatives might find their basis in the cleaner sources of energy like solar, wind, and thermal power, but would be more advanced so that they could completely accommodate our present standard of consumption.) However, this view presupposes a pre-established harmony between what we want (e.g., a certain standard of living and material comfort) and the means by which our desires could be fulfilled via nuclear power:

> If this were so [i.e., that there is no alternative to nuclear energy], it would mean an invisible, intelligent hand would be governing the development of science and technology; that if humanity with its survival and material progress would reach a bottleneck, suddenly the development would be at hand, which alone would enable it to continue with men.[14]

He points out that "as long as . . . the option of nuclear energy is available, there is no urgency that will lead us to alternative solutions."[15] The current level of energy consumption necessary to sustain the West's standard of living and comfort presents a problematic situation because it is unlikely that the West would agree to withhold from using this technology. And, for Spaemann, the problem consists in the fact that we see that there is "no alternative" to the use of nuclear energy even in its "peaceful" form.

In his opinion, the argument for the "peaceful" or "non-peaceful" use of nuclear energy stands or falls based on whether these technologies are in fact "without alternative."[16] Since both arguments are contingent on our desire for a better standard of living at the possible expense of the well-being of others (contemporary or future), on the one hand, and international security with clear winners and losers, on the other hand, nuclear energy cannot be defended from an *ethical perspective*, but only from the perspective of economics, politics, or another non-totalizing viewpoint.[17] From the ethical perspective, according to Spaemann, only one decision would make sense: the decision "to give up the technology of nuclear fission" in order "to preclude catastrophe" definitively. Anything less than this would be an irresponsible gamble with the "elementary resources of life," in his opinion. I would like to examine now the details of Spaemann's ethical argument against the "peaceful" use of nuclear energy.

NUCLEAR ENERGY FROM THE "ETHICAL PERSPECTIVE"

In his essay "Ethical Aspects of Energy Politics" (1980), Spaemann argues that nuclear energy has been considered under many different aspects (economic, international-political, ecological, etc.) but it has never been considered from the ethical perspective.[18] He points out that the ethical perspective "must not arise" in the contemporary debate concerning nuclear energy "because then one would no longer need to name the other aspects. The peculiarity of the ethical aspect is that it brooks no competing standpoint."[19] The ethical aspect subordinates all considerations--economic, political, and so on--to itself and renders a practical judgment about what is good and what is evil. Some people may not be willing to suspend their own interests and view all sides of an issue from an unbiased standpoint; Christians, however, are called to do this based on their profession of faith. For this reason, he believes, Christians make poor partisans since they are willing to suspend their own suppositions and preferences in order to consider all perspectives and sides from an unbiased standpoint, that of the ethical/good.[20] In fact, Christians "are mistrustful of themselves, above all, if their worldview is one of an all-too-pleasing harmony between what they are ready to consider as good, and what is useful, interesting, stimulating, and satisfying to them."[21] To consider the good from the perspective of utility may lead to egregious errors of judgment because such a perspective would be conditioned by what is beneficial to oneself. And it is here that Spaemann insinuates that the issue of nuclear energy has been biased toward a consideration of our benefit without regard to what is good overall.

Since the ethical perspective requires that we consider all the aspects and arguments concerning an issue equally and impartially until the truth has been ascertained, we must have a sense of the "hierarchy of values" and receive a proper education in what is good and evil. Any time that there is a disruption of this sense of hierarchy, says Spaemann, a common cause can be found—namely, "the reluctance or inability to disregard our own particular and momentary interests and so judge our own actions as if they were the actions of another with whom we are concerned." Spaemann calls the ability for such an evaluation "the moral condition of moral behavior[22]."[23] If we are not willing to suspend our own interests, i.e., a concern for what is useful to us, in the consideration of an issue, then we have exchanged the ethical perspective for that of utility: "Failing this [the willingness to consider our actions and those of others impartially], the perspective distorts itself: namely, in that what is pressing or expedient or gratifying to us at the moment appears to us to be generally more valuable or better or more useful than it would be in an impartial consideration."[24] Such a failure results in the current situation of the West in regard to energy consumption: We would like to continue our present standard of living and yet save face before our descendants by claiming that we had "no alternative" but to use nuclear energy. In this way, we construe what is good in terms of what is useful; and, for Spaemann, the useful need not always be the good for *everyone*.[25]

According to Spaemann, our conscious refusal to consider nuclear power from the ethical perspective results from a combined failure on two points: a) that of a consideration of the side-effects of our current actions on those affected; and, b) that of a consideration of the question from the perspective of future generations. We will examine both of these in turn.

SIDE-EFFECTS

In an article he wrote in the late 1970s, during a period in which he was quite vocal in his denunciation of nuclear power, Spaemann makes the following claim:

> Human history is the history of the continual solution of problems arising from the unintended consequences of solutions to past problems. The problem that we have before us, that of the side-effects of purposeful acting, is not new, but nowadays it has reached a new dimension. The long-term absorption of the consequences of human acts by the substructures that are acted upon and which we call nature, appears to be no longer succeeding. The side-effects of human activity have reached proportions that overtask the absorbing capacity of nature.[26]

Under normal conditions—the conditions under which most men have lived in history—there was not the problem that the unintended consequences of our acting would spiral out of control and have the possibility of permanently disrupting the well-being of the natural world. Spaemann explores the question of side-effects of action and this question's relevance to an ethical consideration of nuclear energy in his article "Technological Interventions into Nature as a Problem of Political Ethics" (1979).[27]

Toward the beginning of the article Spaemann draws two important distinctions. He first distinguishes between the "ends/goals"[28] of an action and its unintended consequences: an end is "that consequence which the acting singles out intentionally out of the totality of the consequences of action and in relation to which it reduces all other consequences to side effects, to means or costs."[29] Every action, by its very nature, consists of both the intended consequence chosen by the agent as well as unintended consequences, or "side-effects,"[30] that the agent accepts as the costs of an action. Further, these side-effects must be distinguished from "means"[31] in order to avoid confusion regarding their nature: "means" are "sub-goals"[32] that are "deliberate as such" whereas side-effects are "not known, deliberate, and precipitated" but simply "accepted."[33] An example that Spaemann uses to illustrate these two distinctions derives from war: the destruction of a barracks may be the means to the goal of a military objective, an "end," the destruction of neighboring homes; but a side-effect would be further destruction wrought by using a bomb (e.g., the destruction of a bridge) that could not have been foreseen and was not intended. It is clear that ethics must be concerned with both kinds of ends chosen as well as the means oriented toward the attainment of that end. However, unclear are the criteria by which a side-effect would be considered "reasonable" for the person affected by the action and exactly who would be the bearer of responsibility for "the imposition of the side-effects of an action."

To clarify the criteria of the reasonableness of side-effects, Spaemann examines what he considers to be "two extreme views" on the matter: anarchism and political discourse theory. Although opposite extremes, Spaemann believes they share one common failing: neither can give an adequate account of what would be a reasonable side-effect because, as he puts it in regard to the anarchistic view, "only mature fellow human beings who are alive at the time of the acting can actually agree to the relative consequences of the action".[34] Under both viewpoints, it would be impossible to provide criteria for reasonableness if the voice of those affected is not heard or *cannot* be heard. Justice could not be done since those who are affected by the action could never be given an impartial hearing: this point becomes relevant in Spaemann's consideration of future generations. In this connection, he argues that the individual cannot be the bearer of responsibility for the side-effects of certain actions (such as the activation of nuclear power plants) because action itself depends on partial blindness to the unintended consequences of our acting; instead, the state must bear responsibility. Using discourse analysis, he discusses the role of the state: "Unlike the individual, the state has the duty to see as far as possible with the help of every means available in a definite epoch." However, the state must never consider itself as the entity capable of realizing the greatest ends (which would make it the producer of the greatest side-effects) since it is supposed to fulfill its primary purpose of neutralizing the undesirable side-effects of individual action. Thus, the question of the use of nuclear power must be an issue of "political morals."

According to Spaemann, a consideration of the reasonableness of the side-effects of our interventions[35] into the natural world through our attempts to master it for our own benefit must be evaluated with the knowledge that we are not aware of all possible outcomes. And the state, as the bearer of responsibility in this case, should not decide in favor of the use of nuclear energy because it would burden a group of men (future generations) with new natural constraints that would arise from the danger of radioactive waste (especially in terms of storage and natural disasters). We—the modern, industrialized Western world—are not allowed to consider the issue in terms of probable outcomes for the simple reason that the risks involved do not affect us. Societies are permitted to enter into risks consensually, as in the case of automobile traffic, but only *"as long as those who have taken the risks are the same as those who enjoy the advantages."*[36] Whenever we fly on a plane, we are taking a risk—the plane may crash en route, although such an outcome is improbable. We make a calculation of the risk (or possible side-effect) of flying, but we are the same ones who enjoy the advantage of air travel as those who take the risk of the plane crashing. With nuclear energy, there is a divergence of those who are affected by the calculation of risk and those who would benefit from taking that risk. A consideration of the side-effects of the use of nuclear energy, therefore, necessarily leads to a consideration of the issue from the perspective of those affected, i.e., future generations, to which we shall now turn.

FUTURE GENERATIONS

Our insistence on the "peaceful" use of nuclear power remains conditioned on our consumptive lifestyle in the Western, industrialized world, according to Spaemann. In order to legitimize our use of this volatile source of energy, we try to minimize the risk that something might go wrong: for example, preventative measures against meltdowns as well as security measures to preclude the possibility of terrorist attacks that would use nuclear energy against us. However, all of these measures do not reduce the risk to zero. There is a risk inherent within the technology itself that it might do irreparable damage to what Spaemann calls the "elementary resources of life"—thus, putting natural constraints on future generations that had not been borne hitherto.[37] Even if we minimize the risks as much as possible, it would still be irresponsible to wager the well-being of living things in the future for our own benefit now because we saw that without nuclear power we would have to forego our current standard of living and comfort.

For this reason, Spaemann says the burden of proof in the assessment of the risk of nuclear power lies on the side of those who lobby for its use at present—and not on those, like himself, who question it. In his op-ed piece "After us the meltdown"[38] for the *Frankfurter Allgemeine Zeitung* (October 6, 2006), Spaemann makes the following claim about those who would like the Federal Republic of Germany to reassess the decision to withdraw from nuclear energy:

> Whoever desires to change the existing conditions bears the burden of proof. One does not have to prove

> the reasonableness and rightness of the status quo from scratch each time. He may content himself with explaining the inadmissibility of the opposing arguments. In our case the ones who want to undo the decision to withdraw from nuclear energy production bear the burden of proof.[39]

He calls into question the background assumptions from which these proponents of nuclear energy draw their arguments. The first of these background assumptions concerns the expectation that there will be continuous scientific-technical progress as long as the atomic waste remains radioactive. This would mean that these proponents hold two tacit, interconnected beliefs: 1) even though we have not yet found a safe way to dispose of nuclear waste, there might still be success in the future; and, failing #1, 2) there will be success in keeping this waste from causing harm through safe storage areas. According to Spaemann, both of these beliefs stem from something akin to Leibniz's notion of a "pre-established harmony"—except in this case, this harmony exists between "our needs and the willingness of the universe to fulfill these needs." Expectation that everything will work itself out in regard to waste disposal, or that our descendants will be able to find a solution, equates to what Spaemann calls the "principle of hope."[40]

In an interview conducted shortly after the disaster at the Fukushima-Daiichi nuclear power plant, Spaemann implies that the "principle of hope" is intertwined with the modern consideration of risk. Assessment from this perspective favors freedom/liberty whenever the outcome is unclear.[41] Opposed to this perspective, Spaemann claims that the principle of conservation[42] should always take effect in the calculation of risk: "If the risks, as in this case, become too great, and if they actually create new risks for millennia, the burden of proof lies with the nuclear power lobbyists."[43] Again, this is primarily the risk that the basic resources of life will deteriorate on a planet that would no longer be inhabitable for future generations. In Spaemann's view, the responsible perspective would be that of recognition of a natural prohibition against the free use of nuclear power in its "peaceful" form. We will turn to this shortly.

The second background assumption of the proponents of nuclear energy turns on the supposition that knowledge will continue unabated for the next 10,000 years, the time necessary for the radioactive waste no longer to be dangerous. The proponents believe that the storage sites (see the first assumption) would be inaccessible for this period of time, which presupposes a continuity of knowledge concerning not only the danger of radioactive waste, but even the ability to understand the warning labels affixed before the "No Go Areas."[44] According to Spaemann, there has never been a civilization of that duration in recorded history. What this means is that "the demands for the storage sites must be very high. They must be resistant against every form of flood and against all conceivable geological changes within the required time period."[45] But, even further, the storage sites must be secured from human folly and ignorance—something that Spaemann will touch on in the final background assumption of the nuclear power lobbyists. What this entails would be the division of the planet for coming generations into areas that are habitable and those that are uninhabitable—areas that Spaemann also refers to as "death zones"[46] in order to convey the magnitude of this division.

The last background assumption that Spaemann identifies comes from a consideration of a hypothetical situation that may become an option for the unscrupulous both now and in the future. He writes, "Whoever is not willing to relinquish the aforementioned background beliefs should allow himself to be impressed by the danger that caused Carl Friedrich von Weizsacker to withdraw his earlier argument in favor of nuclear power plants: the danger of terrorism."[47] Spaemann points out that in order to preclude this human danger, Germany (and other nations) would be forced to become a police state. If this were the case, then our present demand for nuclear energy to sustain our current level of comfort in the Western world would require that the world "remain habitable only if all human beings are good."[48] Hence, our freedom to use nuclear energy would constrain the freedom of those in the future to enjoy the goods of the world—i.e., they would be forced into certain areas of the world as well as be forced into definite forms of political association in order to survive. As we can gather from what he says about the ethical perspective, we would not be able to justify the limitation of future generations' freedom and well-being through the continuation of the use of nuclear energy.

NATURAL LAW IN THE ATOMIC AGE

Let us review Spaemann's argument against the use of nuclear energy: He first draws the parallel between the arguments for the "non-peaceful" and "peaceful" uses of nuclear power, whose proponents claim that there is "no alternative" to the use of this power; next, he points out that the argument for the use of nuclear energy rests on considerations that are not ethical since they fail to consider it from the perspective of both those who would benefit from the use of nuclear power as well as those who would be affected by it (future generations); finally, he shows that these arguments do not consider the issue in light of the possible side-effects of the use of nuclear energy on future generations because they assume a "pre-established harmony" between our current desire for comfort in the Western world and that the problem of the disposal of nuclear waste will be resolved in the future. All in all, according to Spaemann, the burden of proof rests on those who argue for the use of nuclear energy because of "the scale and the irreversibility of the damages" on nature "in whose ecological niches life and freedom themselves are located."[49] The ecological crisis of our time has returned us to a point where we acknowledge the natural as antecedent to our freedom to do what we will unreservedly—and thus reverses the Baconian ideal of a "mastery of nature" with the concomitant division of the human from the natural world.[50] Thus, Spaemann's argument turns on the idea that the natural forms a pre-given standard by which to judge whether something is good or bad; in other words, the natural world itself has an "end" that cannot be subordinated to human purpose past, present, or future. It is for this reason that he proposes the general form of the natural law as the point of reference for a decision concerning nuclear energy in his "Foreword" to *Nach uns die Kernschmelze*: "It is sufficient to use our reason to know what is good and what is bad."[51]

Spaemann's renewal of natural law in response to several of the ethical dilemmas in the contemporary world derives from his teleological view of nature and human nature. He affirms this view in one of his most recent addresses: "Natural law rests on the premise that human life, indeed life as such, is part of a normative pattern that derives directly from its nature."[52] In large part, his philosophy begins with a rejection of the "is"/"ought" distinction and other post-Humean positions that derive from the so-called "naturalistic fallacy"—a fallacy which denies that nature (in general) and human nature (in particular) can form the rules for morality. One of the problems that he sees in such a position is that Hume's thesis "rests upon a reductionist notion of being" in which the paradigm for existence is "the corpse" rather than "the life of living things."[53] Inert matter cannot act for itself without being impelled by something else (like Hume's billiard ball example).[54] But, as Spaemann points out repeatedly, this is not how nature should be understood because the natural must be conceived on the basis of the teleologically-oriented living being.

Of course, such a conception cannot simply be an anthropocentric reduction wherein the natural conforms to the structure of the mind. In this anthropocentric view, Spaemann believes that the natural world becomes conceived in terms of human needs:

> One could understand the nurturance of nature in anthropocentric terms. If he destroys nature, man destroys his own basis for existence. If it concerns nature, to that extent it always concerns man. Nevertheless, [. . .] it is necessary to abandon the anthropocentric perspective; for, as long as man interprets nature exclusively as functional for his needs and adjusts his protection of nature from this viewpoint, he will gradually proceed into destruction. He will treat the problem constantly as one of weighing up the choices and each time only leave that of nature which

> allows him to emerge unscathed by such an assessment. With such a case-by-case weighing of choices, the amount of nature is constantly abbreviated.[55]

A functional understanding of nature constitutes one of the hallmarks of Spaemann's reading of modernity—especially, the relation in which the human stands with regard to nature on the whole. The contemporary issue of nuclear energy proceeds on this level as well, for modern human society considers the natural world—down to the most basic unit, the atom—to be at the disposal of human interest. Even those who argue in favor of the conservation of nature tend to do so on the basis of "the quality of the environment" as suited to human "needs": for example, the natural world is to be preserved for the sake of later consumption (either as resource or as nature preserve).[56] Whatever the case, for Spaemann, the human measure stands as *the* measure for the rest of the natural world in the modern functionalist conception of nature.

Nuclear energy highlights the question of the relationship between the human being and the natural world. And in doing so, it raises again the possibility of the natural law approach. In fact, natural law can work as a theory only if an orderly nature underlies human action. As David S. Oderberg writes, "Metaphysics is not enlisted by natural law theory to provide the descriptive premises from which normative conclusions are supposed to flow. On the contrary, natural law theory sees normativity as built into the very fabric of reality in the first place."[57] We do not read off moral rules from "bare facts" in the natural world (which would reiterate the "is"/"ought" distinction); rather, the structure of nature itself provides the guidelines for human activity. If nature were not orderly and purposefully oriented, it would be impossible for the human being to be praised or blamed in his or her actions. Oderberg gives the following example: If we lived in a world where precious metals were the sole currency, and if the nature of these metals were not ordered (e.g., gold unexpectedly turned into lead, and vice-versa), there would be no basis for virtues like generosity, and, therefore, no reason to praise anyone for giving a piece of gold to another person in a time of need. Natural law theory, similarly, presumes that the human being can be rightly ordered and oriented toward the good *because* the natural world itself is so ordered and oriented.

Spaemann has this natural ordering in mind when he says that the discovery of the atomic forces that hold the world together is incredibly important, but that this knowledge has opened a Pandora's box. He considers nuclear energy to harbor within itself an abuse: ". . . it is false when people in the Church say that the technology [nuclear fission] itself is good, it is just that man must not put it to bad use. No: a bad use is already immanent in this technology."[58] One can infer his correction of such a viewpoint from the parallel noted above concerning the "non-peaceful" and "peaceful" uses of nuclear power, for the question does not concern the good or bad purposes to which the technology can be used (i.e., a question of utility).[59] On the contrary, the "bad use" inherent in nuclear fission derives directly from what it does without being set to a specific human purpose: *it divides nature itself and disrupts the cohesive force that binds the universe together—hence, making it intelligible and good*.[60] The division of nature on the smallest level—that of the atom—inevitably leads to the division of nature on larger scales, what Spaemann designates as the division of the planet between inhabitable and uninhabitable zones due to the harmful effects of radiation. The side-effects of the decision to use nuclear energy leads, as we have seen, to tremendous consequences for future generations who must make their own decisions based on a truncated (and, perhaps, dangerous) nature. For this reason, Spaemann always notes the constraint placed on future generations in terms of their ability to choose their own form of political association—i.e., in terms of their freedom.[61]

With the recognition of a nature that exists prior to the freedom of the human, Spaemann believes that the proponents of nuclear energy bear the burden of proof substantiating the "innocuousness" of the use of nuclear energy. Only if all experts have been convinced of its harmlessness can the layman make a clear decision in favor of its use. Since this has not been the case (C.F. von Weizsäcker, as

Spaemann points out, had not been convinced), what this means is that "the activation of nuclear power plants has not been justified ethically..." and, therefore, the state must "induce their deactivation as soon as possible"[62] if already put into use. The harm inherent in the use of nuclear energy, particularly its side-effects for current and future generations when dividing the cohesive force of nature itself, constitutes the reason why Spaemann believes that its use should be forbidden.

CONCLUSION: SPAEMANN'S RENEWAL/EXPANSION OF NATURAL LAW

As we have seen, Spaemann's argument against nuclear energy turns on his understanding of the laws of nature, of which human beings make up a part. In an earlier article on natural law, he makes clear that natural law "*in sensu stricto* implies the claim that freedom is placed into an explicit relation toward its natural conditions, which respects and controls these conditions. In fact, this is valid for nature as the environment just as much as for human nature."[63] So the traditional sense of natural law should include a respect for the natural conditions that make our freedom possible, particularly the environment itself as a natural condition of our acting—although we often tend to overlook a respect for the environment within our actions. As I have shown here, Spaemann's critique of nuclear energy turns on this redefinition of the natural law. His critique, in his view, expands the natural law to apply to areas that had not previously fallen within its purview by returning us to a renewed appreciation of the laws of nature.[64] The situation that we face may be novel, but Spaemann's recommended approach to the situation demands a recollection of nature and its law.[65] Thus, Spaemann's understanding of natural law includes a sense of responsibility for the natural world itself, distinguishing Spaemann's thinking about natural law from that of the traditional conception but also making it controversial. In what remains, I would like to outline how Spaemann's approach fills in the gaps of the earlier Aristotelian/Thomistic conception of natural law that is restricted to rational control of the interpersonal dimension. This is only a first attempt and, hence, by no means exhaustive.

Spaemann, in his essay "Nature," makes the claim that "the primordial mastery of nature ... has now reached a point where it turns against man himself."[66] He continues by noting that the "resources of nature" are "finite," and, therefore, that the survival of the species has become dependent on a "new symbiosis" that is only possible through "conscious remembrance of the natural preconditions of human existence."[67] On the other hand, the expanding dominion of the human being over nature—as promised by Bacon and Descartes at the advent of modernity—results in the increase of the necessity and possibility of the "dominion of man over man." Spaemann thinks that this domination of men over other men is highlighted in the relation between different generations: future generations may inherit a natural world that has been truncated and made dangerous because the "elementary resources of life" have been irreparably damaged.[68] Because we are now capable of endangering these fundamental resources, we are in a position to alter the living conditions of future generations through our collective activity (including, but not limited to, the utilization of nuclear energy). Since the investments in the use of technology have become ever greater over the course of modern history, and these technologies strive toward the complete dominion of the natural world, the "courses which the living set for their descendants" have become "more irreversible."[69] For this reason, then, the natural world has moved "into the sphere of responsibility of human freedom."

For previous thinkers in the natural law tradition (like Aristotle and Aquinas, as well as for their modern counterparts like Locke and Kant), the natural world itself was always assumed to be a given and was incapable of being transformed at will by human hand. Now that the progressive domination of nature through modern science has begun to reach its consummation, and this consummation has revealed a crisis, Spaemann believes that the natural world itself must become a part of our responsibility.[70] And this is necessarily the case because the historical situation has changed due to the goal of progress inherent to the modern project of the mastery of nature. One could say that Spaemann believes that the content of natural law has not changed—we still have the same duties toward our contemporaries as did our ancestors toward theirs—but that our understanding of what's involved in a conception of natural law needs to be greatly expanded.[71] Of course, a renewed appreciation of being/nature would be entailed by such an expansion of natural law. And in this sense Spaemann stands in a long line of German philosophers including Leibniz, Schelling, Heidegger, and, most recently, Hans Jonas. Jonas pointed out that "Being, as it testifies to itself . . . gives tidings not only of what it is, but also of what we owe to it."[72] Both he and Spaemann recognize the inherent obligation toward the natural world because our relation to nature is not one of "despotic subjugation," but rather one of interdependence. In Spaemann's own words, what is necessary today is not the act of planning to eradicate undesirable side-effects of our activities, but rather the act of "letting-be"[73] so that nature can stand forth as valuable in itself.[74]

NOTES

1. An earlier version of this paper was presented at the 17th annual meeting of the International Association for Environmental Philosophy in Eugene, Oregon. I thank David Storey and Theresa Morris for inviting me to present at the conference; and I especially thank Alexander Schimpf and January Simpson for comments on drafts of my paper.

2. Holger Zaborowski, *Robert Spaemann's Philosophy of the Human Person: Nature, Freedom, and the Critique of Modernity* (Oxford: Oxford University Press, 2010), 62. Cf. also Spaemann's "Aquinas Medalist Address" at the recent meeting of the American Catholic Philosophical Association: "Why There Is No Law without Natural Law," trans. Tobias Hoffmann, *Proceedings of the American Catholic Philosophical Association: Philosophy in the Abrahamic Traditions* 86 (2012): 17-22.

3. Cf. Robert Spaemann, "Unter welchen Umständen kann man noch von Fortschritt sprechen?" in *Philosophische Essays, Erweiterte Ausgabe* (Stuttgart: Reclam, 1994), 140, where Spaemann notes that the goal of modern science is not the "mastery of what is lower by what is higher," but rather the "despotic

subjugation of nature through that of progressive objectification and de-naturing." All translations from *Philosophische Essays* are my own.

4. Cf. Robert Spaemann, *Nach uns die Kernschmelze: Hybris im atomaren Zeitalter* (Stuttgart: Klett-Cotta, 2011). All translations from this work are those of Gregory Canning and Alexander Schimpf.

5. Spaemann, *Nach uns*, 7. In many ways, Spaemann's reflections on nuclear power echo the concerns that Hans Jonas gave voice to in his work *The Imperative of Responsibility: In Search of an Ethics for the Technological Age* (Chicago: University of Chicago Press, 1984).

6. keine Alternative

7. Spaemann, *Nach uns*, 9. Emphasis added.

8. Cf. Robert Spaemann, *Grenzen: Zur ethischen Dimension des Handelns* (Stuttgart: Klett-Cotta, 2001).

9. Spaemann, *Nach uns*, 9-10.

10. Spaemann, "Brief an Heinrich Böll" in *Grenzen*, 321.

11. ohne Alternative.

12. Brückentechnologie.

13. Spaemann, *Nach uns*, 8.

14. Ibid.

15. Ibid.

16. ohne Alternative.

17. Cf., for an elucidation of the notion of a "conditional good," Robert Spaemann, *Basic Moral Concepts*, trans. T.J. Armstrong (New York/London: Routledge, 1989), pp. 1-3.

18. Cf. Robert Spaemann, "Ethische Aspekte der Energiepolitik," in *Nach uns*, pp. 49-69.

19. Spaemann, *Nach uns*, 49-50.

20. Elsewhere—especially in the context of discussing human dignity—Spaemann makes the argument that the ethical overlaps with a disinterested consideration of what is good overall: "Human dignity [. . .] is not subject to compromises. Even when rights are going to be limited, this dignity will insist that, with regard to the considerations of justice that demand or allow these limitations, the question must be asked whether the interests of those whose rights are so limited are impartially taken into account." Robert Spaemann, "Human Dignity and Human Nature", in *Love and the Dignity of Human Life: On Nature and Natural Law* (Grand Rapids, MI/ Cambridge, UK: William B. Eerdmans Publishing Company, 2012), 42-43. Cf. also Robert Spaemann, *Basic Moral Concepts*, 26-28.

21. Spaemann, *Nach uns*, 52.

22. moralische Voraussetzung sittlichen Verhaltens.

23. Ibid., 55.

24. Ibid., 56.

25. Richard Schenk also points out this feature of our thinking, which Spaemann critiques in our use of nuclear energy: "The lack of a bad conscience, far from making acts against environmental conservation good, is part of the problem. Spaemann identifies the current culture of disposable goods as a typical example of functionalism: the goods of creation have become mere 'resources,' not irreplaceable goods in themselves. They are called goods only insofar as they are seen to be instrumental to another good, which itself is only good as instrumental to another, and so on." Richard Schenk, O.P., "The Ethics of Robert Spaemann,"

in *One Hundred Years of Philosophy*, ed. Brian J. Shanley, O.P. (Washington, D.C.: The Catholic University of America Press, 2001), 162.
26. Robert Spaemann, "Side-Effects as a Moral Problem", trans. Frederick S. Gardiner, in *Contemporary German Philosophy*, Vol. 2, eds. Darrel E. Christensen, Manfred Riedel, Robert Spaemann, Reiner Wiehl, Wolfgang Wieland (University Park/London: The Pennsylvania State University Press, 1983), 139.
27. Cf. Robert Spaemann, "Technische Eingriffe in die Natur als Problem der politischen Ethik", in *Nach uns*, pp. 13-48.
28. Zwecke.
29. Spaemann, *Nach uns*, 14.
30. Nebenwirkungen.
31. Mitteln.
32. Unterzwecke.
33. Ibid.
34. Ibid., 19.
35. Eingriffe.
36. Ibid., 40. Emphasis added. This would also be the reason why he sees that discourse theory fails to address the issue of nuclear energy appropriately.
37. "[...] coming generations will not forgive us if we, for the first time in the history of humanity, consciously and deliberately bequeath to them new natural constraints, only because we have falsely presented our social problems as factual and natural constraints. They will say that the social, economic, and political problems that we had were quasi-natural constraints, while they had real natural constraints that could no longer be displaced or transformed at will." Spaemann, *Nach uns*, 67. Cf., also, Spaemann "Unter welchen Umständen...", pp. 149-150.
38. Cf. Robert Spaemann, "Nach uns die Kernschmelze" in *Nach uns*, pp. 86-90.
39. Spaemann, *Nach uns*, 86.
40. das Prinzip Hoffnung.
41. in dubio pro libertate.
42. in dubio pro reo, in dubio pro vita.
43. Spaemann's phrase recalls Ernst Bloch's work *Das Prinzip Hoffnung* (1959), a book that contained a utopian outlook of progress that Hans Jonas critiqued in his own major work of ethics, *Das Prinzip Verantwortung* (1979)—the original title in German of *The Imperative of Responsibility*. Spaemann himself was greatly impressed with Jonas's work as is clear from Jonas's reflections in his *Memoirs* (2008). Cf., for a fuller discussion of the relation between these works, Michael Löwy, "Ernst Bloch's Prinzip Hoffnung and Hans Jonas's Prinzip Verantwortung", trans. Margret Vince, in *The Legacy of Hans Jonas: Judaism and the Phenomenon of Life*, eds. Hava Tirosh-Samuelson and Christian Wiese (Leiden/Boston: Brill, 2010), pp. 149-158.
44. Spaemann, "Die Vernunft, das Atom und der Glaube: Über entfesselte Wissenschaft, frivole Wachstumspolitik und das verdrängte Restrisiko", *Nach uns*, 104.
45. Elsewhere, Spaemann notes that there is only one "area of continuous progress, that of the area of written, fixable, positive knowledge," and calls this idea of "progress in the singular" into question over and over. Spaemann, "Unter welchen Umständen...", 138.
46. Todeszonen.

47. Spaemann, *Nach uns*, 88. Cf., most recently, Spaemann on the passage of time (albeit in a different context): "Time is not creative. Its passage does not restore lost innocence. In fact, its tendency is always just the opposite—namely, to increase entropy. Every instance of order in nature is wrested from the grip of entropy and over time eventually falls under its dominion once again." Robert Spaemann, "Divorce and Remarriage", *First Things*, August/September 2014, 18.
48. Spaemann, *Nach uns*, 90.
49. Ibid.
50. Spaemann, *Nach uns*, 47.
51. Cf. Holger Zaborowski, "Nature—Reason—Freedom. Thinking about Natural Law in Modern Philosophy", trans. Gregory Canning, in *Human Rights and Natural Law: An Intercultural Philosophical Perspective*, ed. Walter Schweidler (Sankt Augustine: Academia, 2012), pp. 20-35.
52. Spaemann, *Nach uns*, 11.
53. Spaemann, "Why There Is No Law without Natural Law", 19. Cf. also Zaborowski, *Robert Spaemann's Philosophy*, 64.
54. Ibid.
55. "Nature [in the modern scientific conception] is rendered an immanent realm where objects are merely moved, a realm of inert matter preserving itself. Nature becomes exteriority without selfhood (Selbstsein)." Robert Spaemann, "Human Nature," in *Essays in Anthropology: Variations on a Theme*, trans. Guido de Graaff and James Mumford (Eugene, OR: Cascade Books, 2010), 9.
56. Spaemann, *Nach uns*, 36-37.
57. "[...] we can reflect about which parts of nature, which landscapes, which fauna and flora we would like to preserve because we enjoy them. But when we correlate nature in this way immediately to what is convenient for the human being, we are already on the wrong path." Robert Spaemann, "Naturteleologie und Handlung", in *Philosophische Essays, Erweiterte Ausgabe* (Stuttgart: Reclam, 1994), 54.
58. David S. Oderberg, "The Metaphysical Foundations of Natural Law" in *Natural Moral Law in Contemporary Society*, ed. Holger Zaborowski (Washington, DC: The Catholic University of America Press, 2010), 45.
59. Spaemann, *Nach uns*, 105.
60. This is why Spaemann says, reflecting back on the nuclear arms race, "At that time, I regarded an American monopoly on atomic weapons to be just as dangerous as a Soviet one." Spaemann, *Nach uns*, 10.
61. Cf., also, Robert Spaemann, "Natur", in *Philosophische Essays, Erweiterte Ausgabe* (Stuttgart: Reclam, 1994), p. 35, where he states that "Nature is experienced in acting as an order of things which is not amenable to influence in its fundamental laws by acting, but, conversely, offers dependability precisely because of its regularity, without which no purpose could be realized through action."
62. Cf., Spaemann, "Unter welchen Umständen...," 149.
63. Spaemann, *Nach uns*, 47-48.
64. Robert Spaemann, "Die Aktualität des Naturrechts", in *Philosophische Essays, Erweiterte Ausgabe* (Stuttgart: Reclam, 1994), 75.
65. It should be noted that Spaemann insists that the natural law is not simply a teaching limited to Christianity, as many of its detractors suggest. Spaemann views nature and the natural law as ubiquitously recognized in various cultures: "Whatever progress mankind makes in moral matters is only possible because of

an unchanging standard: the very same standard which the Greeks called physis, the Chinese tradition called Tao, and the biblical tradition called the 'will of God'." Spaemann, "Why There is No Law Without Natural Law," 20. Cf., also, Spaemann, "Die Aktualität des Naturrechts", 63, where he states that the natural law is not simply an "occidental order of values" or a "system of values that underlies our constitution," for in both cases the natural law would be merely a Western phenomenon (i.e., relative to a single culture).

66. Cf. Zaborowski, *Robert Spaemann's Philosophy*, pp. 56-68. Zaborowski puts it this way: "Philosophy is, in Spaemann's view, primarily the free recollection of nature."

67. Robert Spaemann, "Natur", 36.

68. Ibid., 36-37.

69. Cf., especially, Robert Spaemann, *Basic Moral Concepts*, pp. 88-89, where Spaemann alludes to the ecological crisis while noting that the obligations of the earlier generations are greater than those of future generations. It is one of the tasks of the earlier generation to hand on "an inheritance" [the natural world] that has not been "decimated and plundered." He implies that the natural world has become a medium for the "friendship between generations."

70. Robert Spaemann, "Unter welchen Umständen. . .," 149.

71. Cf. Robert Spaemann, "Ende der Modernität?" in *Philosophische Essays, Erweiterte Ausgabe* (Stuttgart: Reclam, 1994), pp. 247-260.

72. This is a point to which Hans Jonas has called attention: "Modern technology has introduced actions of such novel scale, objects, and consequences that the framework of former ethics can no longer contain them. [. . .] To be sure the old prescriptions of the 'neighbor' ethics—of justice, charity, honesty, and so on—still hold in their intimate immediacy for the nearest, day-by-day sphere of human interaction. But this sphere is overshadowed by a growing realm of collective action where doer, deed, and effect are no longer the same as they were in the proximate sphere, and which by the enormity of its powers forces upon ethics a new dimension of responsibility never dreamed of before." Hans Jonas, *Imperative of Responsibility*, 6.

73. Seinlassen

74. Hans Jonas, *Philosophische Untersuchungen und metaphysische Vermutungen* (Frankfurt am Main: Insel Verlag, 1992), 130.

75. Robert Spaemann, "Naturteleologie und Handlung," 54. Cf., also, Robert Spaemann, "Ich plädiere für die Rückkehr zu einem Fortschritt im Plural," *Nach uns*, 81, where he emphasizes that Heidegger's concept of freedom as "letting-be" [Sein-Lassen] is "better understood today than at the time when he [Heidegger] expressed it" in light of the ecological crisis.

NATURAL LAW FROM A CATHOLIC-MUSLIM PERSPECTIVE: A COMPARATIVE STUDY OF JACQUES MARITAIN'S AND ABDULLAHI AHMED AN-NA'IM'S PHILOSOPHY OF LAW

Paola Bernardini

In recent years the study of natural law has gained new momentum, not only within the Catholic tradition, but also within and across different religious denominations. New impulse to the cross-cultural study of natural law has been advocated, amongst others, by the International Theological Commission (ITC) assembled by the Holy See to examine doctrinal questions. In the year 2008, ITC issued a document called "The Search for Universal Ethics: New Look at the Natural Law." "In this document"–its subscribers wrote–"we intend to invite all who ask themselves about the ultimate foundations of ethics and of the juridical and political order, to consider the resources that a renewed presentation of the teaching of the natural law contains .... Christianity does not have a monopoly on the natural law. In fact, the natural law, founded on reason, which is common to all human beings, is the basis for collaboration between all men of good will, beyond their religious convictions."[1] Attempts to give impulse to the cross-cultural study of natural law have also come from North American scholars, namely Anver Emon, Matthew Levering and David Novak, who have recently coedited a volume under the title *Natural Law: a Jewish, Christian and Muslim Trialogue* (Oxford: Oxford University Press, 2014). Their contention, as that of the others, is that natural law can provide a plausible common ground for citizens of different faiths to start reasoning together about the public good in a pluralist society. Such an endeavor is not irrelevant if one considers that eight-in-ten people living in the world today identify with a religious group. Of these, the majority are Christians, followed by Muslims.[2]

However, natural law can take different forms and shapes even within the same tradition. That is why in my own cross-cultural research, I have focused on the specific philosophy of law of two modern authors–Jacques Maritain and Abdullahi Ahmed An-Na'im–belonging respectively to the Catholic and Islamic tradition.[3] As many scholars trained in the West know, Jacques Maritain wrote over sixty books, many of which are on the subject of natural law and the rights of man. His philosophy of rights, grounded on Thomas Aquinas' natural law, exercised a great influence on the preparatory works of the United Nations' Universal Declaration of Human Rights.[4] On the other hand, not many know about the work of the contemporary Muslim jurist Abdullahi Ahmed An-Na'im, whom I like to call "the Maritain of Islam." Having fled from Sudan in the 1990's during the consolidation of the fundamentalist regime of Hassan al-Turabi, An-Na'im was named Charles Howard Candler Professor of Law at Emory Law School in 1999. Not only has he extensively written on the subject of Islamic law reform and universal human rights, but his books have also had an impact in the Muslim world, judging from the existing translations in Farsi, Arabic and Indonesian and from the fact that his books are required texts in various universities of Southeast Asia.[5]

In what follows, I will present the summary of my findings starting with the separate presentation of each author's contributions followed by a discussion of their similarities and differences.

JACQUES MARITAIN'S THOMISTIC ACCOUNT OF THE NATURAL LAW

Jacques Maritain's foremost contribution to natural law theory lies in the critique of the Enlightenment interpretations of the doctrine of natural law. During the "rationalist era" – as he calls the Enlightenment – jurists and philosophers had so misused the notion of natural law to make it either appear useless for ethical decision-making or frowned upon with suspicion by non-Western scholars.[6] Accordingly, "natural law was conceived after the pattern of a written code, applicable to all, of which any just law should be transcription, and which would determine a-priori and in all its aspects the norms of human behaviour through ordinances supposedly prescribed by Nature and Reason, but in reality arbitrarily and artificially formulated."[7] Counteracting these tendencies, Maritain develops and brings back to life again the Aristotelian-Thomistic account of natural law. Like Aristotle, he defines natural law as the "normality of functioning" of each and every living being.[8] Just like all pianos have as their ends the productions of determinate sounds, Maritain argues, men have as their own constitutive ends the production of certain actions–the pursuit of which fulfils their normality of functioning. Natural law is nothing more or less than the sum of unwritten principles and precepts which guide the human person toward one's given ends. As such it is a non-codified, existential law, which – as Aquinas already wrote – bears the imprint of Divine Reason.[9] Moreover, it can be discovered only gradually, through trial and error, relying on the more or less precise rationalization of human experience, especially of the "natural inclinations" with which God has endowed men.[10] In this respect, the study of natural law can benefit both from the contribution of historical critique and ethnography, as Maritain acknowledges in his *Loi naturelle ou loi non ecrite*.[11]

Another major contribution of Maritain's natural law theory lies in its differentiation of the moral from the juridical aspect of natural law. More often than not, Maritain uses natural law interchangeably to refer both to the natural law of morality and to the natural law of justice. But he is deeply aware of their difference, and in one instance at least, he even refers to them with the separate terms of "natural law" (*loi naturelle*) and "natural right" (*droit naturelle*) respectively:

> Natural Law which is not written .... concerns man as man, and a community which is neither the body politic nor the civilized community but simply the community of the human species and .... obliges us in conscience .... It concerns the moral, not the juridical order. What we have

> here is nothing other than the notion of debitum morale, of that which is morally due by virtue of right reason ...., but not by virtue of juridical constraint. How then under these conditions can we speak of natural right? ... would it not be preferable to rid oneself of such an expression? This is a temptation of the philosopher .... Nevertheless, I do not believe that we must yield to it .... For in a considerably more profound and universal sense, it is necessary to say that each man bears within himself the judiciary authority of humanity....and consequently, the right of imposing constraint which derives from this authority .... which goes back to the Author of nature and humanity.[12]

According to Maritain, the existence of a natural law of justice becomes evident when "States, in the absence of an international judiciary power, have recourse to sanctions such as war or just reprisals against the aggression of another State, or against the barbarous procedures it employs."[13] It is also manifest when someone, in the absence of a judge, justifiably asserts the right to self-defence when attacked by another man. Similarly, one could not protest against a missed restitution of debt if one did not already have a natural sense that all debts must be paid back, or that one has the right to such restitution.[14]

The differentiation between the moral and juridical aspects of natural law does not go without practical implications. If the role of the State is to promote justice, then such differentiation limits the scope of natural law which can be enforced by the State:

> Doubtless ... the State has the right to punish me if, my conscience being blind, I follow my conscience and commit an act in itself criminal or unlawful. But in like circumstances the State has not the authority to make me reform the judgement of my conscience, any more than it has the power of imposing upon intellects its own judgement of good and evil.[15]

Secondly, it also follows that the natural rights, grounded on natural law, are differentiated accordingly as moral or juridical,[16] the former being the object of the common good of morality and the latter being the object of governance, or the State.

THE DYNAMISM OF NATURAL LAW

The unwritten, existential law—which Maritain calls natural law—comprises very basic principles and derivative precepts. While the former basic principles[17] are self-evident in virtue of the concepts involved,[18] the derivative norms of natural law which follow therefrom may be more or less manifest, depending on the level of moral awareness achieved.[19] This explains why the knowledge of natural law involves a dynamic development and continues to progress as long as human history endures.

In the pre-reflective stage, natural inclinations present themselves in the disguise of "dynamic schemes of action" such as "To take a man's life is not like taking another animal's life," or "The family group has to comply with some fixed pattern," or "Sexual intercourse has to be contained within given limitations," or "We are bound to live together under certain rules and prohibitions."[20] These dynamic schemes are more universally shared than what it is normally believed, due to their spontaneity and indeterminacy. Not so the "common law of civilization" or "law of nations"[21] that derives from an effort at rational conceptualization and includes precepts such as "Thou shall not kill," "Thou shall not steal," "Honor thy father and thy mother," "Thou shall not commit adultery." These precepts may not be always acknowledged for different reasons and even if they were they would still require further determination in order to provide guidance for action. Maritain gives the classical example of giving back to the owner the goods held in trust. Due to their perverted conscience, some ancient people did not think that giving back the goods held in trust was the right thing to do. Others did not apply this maxim, and rightly so, when their owner sought to do evil by recourse to these same goods.

The common law of civilization coincides with the second table of the Decalogue, supporting the argument in favour of the intelligibility of Judeo-Christian Revelation. Not surprisingly, the medieval jurist Gratian, quoted by Aquinas, used to say that natural law is the law contained in the Old and New Testament.[22] However, this law—as already mentioned—is still quite undetermined and needs to be further specified according to the degree of moral awareness attained.[23] Maritain gives the example of adultery. Its prohibition was interpreted differently by the Patriarchs. Abraham, Osea and the Jewish people used to marry more than one wife. In this case, as Thomas Aquinas already taught, Maritain believes that they were not acting against a fundamental precept of natural law or of the Decalogue –"Do not commit adultery"– but only against its specific determination. Similarly, "Divorce or repudiation of the spouse was sometimes permitted by Moses .... Now, divorce is totally and completely forbidden by the New Law .... As the Gospel reads: 'Because of the hardness of your hearts Moses allowed you to divorce your wives, but from the beginning it was not so.' In both these cases, due to a still crepuscular moral conscience, God released some people from a second precept of the natural law."[24]

FROM NATURAL LAW TO NATURAL RIGHTS

No matter how clear or crepuscular the knowledge of the natural law may be, according to the French philosopher, it can still provide a normative model for the law of the State and a solid foundation for human rights. As a matter of fact, the principles and precepts of the natural law, Maritain continues, do "not prescribe merely things to be done and not to be done: they also recognize rights, in particular rights linked to the very nature of man."[25] So it is that "the same natural law which lays down our fundamental duties ... is the very law which assigns our fundamental rights."[26] Maritain acknowledges that neither Aristotle nor Aquinas ever talked of rights as subjective claims. "In ancient and medieval times," rather, "attention was paid, in natural law, to the obligations of man more than to his rights." Unfortunately, Maritain continues, modernity has now shifted its focus from natural obligations to rights only, leading to a clash of absolutes. However, "a genuine and comprehensive view," brought about by progress in moral conscience, "would pay attention both to the obligations and rights involved in the requirements of natural law."[27]

Maritain provides some examples of rights required by the natural law in both its juridical and ethical dimension. However, like the notion of natural law, he uses the term natural rights interchangeably to refer to either subjective moral claims–i.e. the right to the pursuit of the perfection of moral life,[28] the right to fulfil one's destiny,[29] the right to the pursuit of eternal good, the right to choose the true path[30]–or to subjective juridical claims such as the right to an equal share of material goods, or the right to profess, without interference by the state, any religious path whatsoever.[31] In the first case, natural rights are determined by what is truly good and necessary for each, in the sense of truly conductive to his moral perfection or integral flourishing. In the second, they are determined by reference to what is necessary to establish a just order of relationships.

ABDULLAHI AHMED AN-NA'IM'S AND THE ISLAMIC TRADITION OF "NATURAL LAW"

Scholars of Islam generally agree that natural law is also part of the rationalist Muslim tradition since the time of Mu'tazilites' theology and the philosophy of Ibn Rushd (Averroes).[32] The Mu'tazilah, who lived in the Abbasy period (eighth and ninth centuries), believed that "nature is invested with a presumptive normativity that stems from God's purposeful creation." [33] In their view, there was no need of Revelation to know that the good must be done and that the evil must be avoided. This was a principle whose validity and knowability is based on the divinely endowed dispositions of human reason. For his part, Averroes welcomed Greek philosophy, especially in the realm of jurisprudence, as a way of making intelligible the Law of God found in the sacred texts of Islam. In the "Middle Commentary" of Aristotle's *Nicomachean Ethics*, for example, Averroes argued for the necessity of the human legislator to adapt with equity the Islamic law on jihad (holy war): Since "the Muslim masses make this edict of war generally valid despite the impossibility of destroying their enemies completely ...," Averroes writes, "great damage has attained them on account of their ignorance of the intention of the Lawgiver."[34]

While the Muʿtazilites' justified the validity of ethical norms in light of the divinely bestowed dispositions of reason, Averroes aimed to show the intelligibility of the law of God in light of its equity. In time, Abdulaziz Sachedina writes, this rationalist tradition in Islam "was defeated by Ash'arite divine command traditionalism" which became then prevalent, but it has recently "resurfaced among Sunni Muslim modernists and continues to influence their advocacy of human rights" today.[35] One case in point is Abdullahi Ahmed An-Na im's human rights theory, which is grounded on what he calls the "common normative principles" of humanity.

THE COMMON PRINCIPLES AND NORMS OF HUMANITY

According to An-Naʿim, there are two "common normative principles shared by all the major cultural traditions."[36] One is the principle which accords that man needs to be treated like an end, never as a means.[37] The other is the principle of reciprocity, which enjoins that one should treat other people as he or she wishes to be treated by them. These principles do not concern the relation of the individual with the Creator, which is more a matter of private worship. Rather they concern the relation of the individual with the State and society. An-Na'im also acknowledges that the Golden Rule–which is another way of saying that if I want to be treated as an end in myself, I should also treat others in the same way–is something that one can find in many verses both of the Qur'an and Sunna.[38] However, what makes it valid is not the fact that it can be found in the Qur'an but rather its universal acknowledgement.[39]

These common universal principles, An-Na'im continues, have been applied differently across time and space: "Cultural, and particularly religious, traditions" have historically restricted "the application of the principle [of reciprocity] to other members of its cultural or religious tradition, if not to a certain group of people within a given tradition."[40] For instance, "the historical conception of the principle of reciprocity under Shari'a did not apply to women and non-Muslims to the same extent that it applied to Muslim men."[41] While women were not allowed to marry more than one husband, men were allowed to marry more than one woman. This differential treatment was justified by the circumstances of the time. In fact, "in the historical context of Shari'a, women were dependent on men for their security and economic well-being. Since men were in short supply because of the ravages of war in the seventh century, it was better for a woman to share a husband with other cowives than to remain a destitute and defenceless spinster."[42] However, "while such aspects of Shari'a represented significant improvements on political and legal systems that prevailed throughout the pre-modern world, they are totally unacceptable from a constitutional point of view today."[43]

This dialectic between the universality and contingency of the common principles is also referred to by An-Na'im with the notion of "weak cultural relativism." According to this view, "morality may be universal in the sense that all cultures have it, but that does not in any way indicate the content of that morality."[44] At the same time, weak cultural relativism does not "reject all universal criteria," nor does it rest content with "the existing least common denominator."[45] This would be in fact equal to espousing the strong cultural relativist position.

What this dialectic of universality and contingency amounts to is the necessity of the human legislator to derive specific norms of conduct from the universal principles and norms while paying attention to the context. According to An-Na'im, "we have a sea of normativity–don't lie, don't cheat, don't oppress others, and don't attack others violently–these are our ethical norms [....] But out of that, the State, the people who run the State–those who have been elected–try to find a legal response to new questions, like for instance cloning, or artificial insemination, or organ transplant. So we have an ethical source from which we need to derive a legal rule."[46] This is a secular law, or as Maritain would put it, a positive law grounded on natural principles.

FROM "NATURAL LAW" TO "NATURAL RIGHTS"

By applying common principles and norms to the "fundamental interests, concerns, qualities and traits" of humanity, An-Na'im also believes that "we can identify those rights, claims and entitlements that ought to be protected as human rights even if they are not to be identified (…) by any formal document."[47] As such, they constitute the standard criteria of the Bill of Rights included in national Constitutions, or in International Covenants of Human Rights,[48] so much so that human rights are not "accepted as universal simply because they are recognized [...] by the(se) documents."[49] To take this stance would amount to espousing a "positivist view of human rights."[50] Rather, "the rights are recognized by the documents because they are universal human rights."[51]

Even though An-Na'im rarely, if ever, uses this term, one could dare say that, for the reasons outlined above, universal human rights are equivalent to Maritain's "natural" rights. More specifically they are equivalent to Maritain's natural justice claims in as much as they are defined as "the rights of the individual against the State and society at large,"[52] or as those "legal entitlements which are due to all human beings, without such distinction on such grounds as race, sex (gender), or religion."[53] Their logic, or rationale, is not based on religious morality but rather on public morality. Unlike more traditional Muslim thinkers, he avoids using the notion of divine rights (huquq Allah). In his view, this notion is problematic inasmuch as "when you say that a right is the right of God you are actually saying it is non-enforceable. Because if it is God's right, then only God can enforce it (presumably in the afterlife)."[54]

The thorough application of the common principles of humanity to the "fundamental interests, concerns, qualities and traits" of humanity should even lead Muslims "to establish a technique for reinterpreting the basic sources (of shari'a), the Quran and Sunna, in a way that would enable us to remove the basis of discrimination against women and non-Muslims."[55] Of course, in order to meet this objective, the principle of reciprocity itself should be construed in an "enlightened" way such that it would pass the test of universalizability. First of all, in accord with the equal dignity of all, it should "extend the 'other person' to all human beings, regardless of gender, religion, race or language."[56] Second, it should not be taken to imply that one's perceptions have to be imposed on the other. For example, "it should not be open to a Muslim to say that since he accepts Islamic law, or Shari'a, for himself, he would conform with the principle of reciprocity in imposing Shari'a on non-Muslims" living in an Islamic state. Rather, the principle of reciprocity requires that one tries to put oneself in the position of the other person, imagining what rights would one demand for oneself were he or she in the place of another religious minority: "Since a Muslim would demand the right to decide what law should apply to him or her and would not accept being subjected to the religious law of non-Muslims, he or she should grant the same right to non-Muslims."[57] Finally, the principle of reciprocity should not be confused with mere retaliation, or negative reciprocity. "In other words, X should not be entitled to deny Y's rights on the grounds that Y is unlikely to afford X the same rights."[58]

COMMONALITIES AND DIFFERENCES

Unlike Maritain, An-Na'im seldom, if ever, uses the term "natural law" to refer to the universal laws of morality or justice. Rather he prefers to refer to it with such terms as, for instance, "common normative principle shared by all the major cultural traditions"[59] in virtue of the "fundamental interests, concerns, qualities, traits, and values"[60] shared by humanity. One reason for such avoidance may be that he does not want to foster illicit identifications between the Islamic and Western traditions of the natural law. As Maritain puts it, "the doctrines of natural law, like any other political and legal doctrines may propound various arguments or theories in order to substantiate or justify natural law."[61] Likewise, An-Na'im acknowledges that "there is not only a basic similarity in the notion of 'natural law' in the Islamic and Western traditions but also significant differences due to the various theological and legal resources deployed in support of the idea."[62]

These differences are also evident in An-Na'im's and Maritain's justifications of the theistic nature of the natural law. While both scholars consider natural law as based on the divinely endowed, common rationality of humanity, they offer different justifications for their statement. Maritain, like Aquinas, argues for the theistic nature of the natural law on philosophical, more precisely epistemological and ethical grounds. Since "human reason has no share in its establishment, but only in its knowledge," Maritain writes at one point, "natural law must be the product of Divine Reason."[63] Moreover, Maritain argues, "Natural Law obliges by virtue of Eternal Law." In fact, "if God does not exist, the Natural Law lacks obligatory Power."[64] Men would lack any moral motivation to act in accordance with its dictates.

On his part, An-Na'im affirms the theistic nature of "natural law" on scriptural grounds. It is the compatibility with the universal principles contained in the sacred scripture and oral tradition of Islam which accounts for its being ultimately rooted in divine law. In this sense, while both Maritain's and An-Na'im's theories may be defined as ultimately theistic, they are so for different reasons.

Despite the theoretical and terminological differences, both An-Na'im and Maritain would be ready to admit that, as a matter of fact, their similarities may be more prevalent. Maritain writes, "Men possessing quite different, even opposite metaphysical or religious outlooks, can converge, not by virtue of any identity of doctrine, but by virtue of an analogical similitude in practical principles, toward the same practical conclusions."[65] This convergence, in fact, would testify to the existence of natural apperceptions, or inclinations, which may or may not be expressed identically. Likewise, An-Na'im admits that in the practical realm, the implications of the natural law doctrines may be more terminological than substantial.[66]

From the practical point of view, for example, the similarity between An-Na'im's and Maritain's theories seems to lie in the superior, normative role that natural law plays with respect to, on the one hand, the public laws of the State and, on the other, the religious norms contained in the Bible or the Qur'an. In the same way that Maritain judges the Mosaic law on polygamy as surpassed by a more modern understanding of the exigencies of natural law, An-Na'im interprets the Qur'anic rules on polygamy as contingent to the time and place of the prophet Muhammad and contrary to enlightened understanding of reciprocity.

Finally, both Maritain and An-Na'im draw similar conclusions also from the distinction between natural justice and natural morality, a distinction neither irrelevant nor obvious. It is certainly not obvious for some traditionalist Muslim scholars who either ignore the concept of human rights altogether, preferring to rely on the idea of the rights of God (huquq Allah), or, if they use it at all, narrow it down to its moral rather than juridical meaning. For instance, they recognize the moral claim to pursue the truth but do not likewise recognize the right not to be coerced by the State in the pursuit of this truth[67] which can lead the State to distinguish true from false religious claims, impinging on the religious liberty of its citizens.

NOTES

1. International Theological Commission, *The Search for Universal Ethics: New Look at the Natural Law: Introduction*, § 9, 11.
2. Pew Research Center Report, *The Global Religious Landscape*, (December 2012), http://www.pewforum.org/2012/12/18/global-religious-landscape-exec/
3. Paola Bernardini, Abdullahi Ahmed An-Na'im's *Human Rights Theory and Jacques Maritain's Natural Law Theory: A Comparative Study*, (PhD diss., Pontifical University St. Thomas Aquinas, 2012).
4. Jacques Maritain was one of the participants to the United Nations Educational, Scientific, and Cultural Organization (UNESCO) Symposium of Philosophers, held in early 1948 with the goal of drafting an "International Declaration of Human Rights." The results and comments of this Symposium were published later that year, with an "Introduction" by Jacques Maritain, in UNESCO, Human Rights. Comments and Interpretations, July 25 1948.
5. *Islam and the Secular State: Negotiating the Future of Shari'a* (Cambridge: Harvard University Press, 2008) has been published in Indonesian (2007) and in Arabic (2010). Chapters of this book are also available in Urdu,

Turkish, Farsi, and Bengali on An-Na'im's personal website at Emory University; *Toward an Islamic Reformation: Civil Liberties, Human Rights and International Law* (Syracuse: Syracuse University Press, 1990) has been translated and published in Arabic and Indonesian (1995), Russian (1999), Farsi (2003), Italian (2011).

6. Maritain, *Man and the State*, (Washington D.C.: The Catholic University of America Press, 1998), 81.
7. Ibid., 82-83.
8. Ibid., 86.
9. Thomas Aquinas, ST Ia IIae, q. 15-16; Maritain, "Natural Law and Moral Law," in *Moral Principles of Action*, ed. Ruth Nanda Anshen, (New York: Harper & Brothers, 1952), 65-66.
10. Following Aquinas, Maritain describes knowledge by inclination as "a kind of knowledge that is not clear, like that obtained through concepts and conceptual judgments. It is obscure, unsystematic, vital knowledge by means of instinct or sympathy, and in which the intellect, in order to make its judgments, consults inner leanings of the subject." Jacques Maritain, *Natural Law. Reflections on Theory and Practice*, ed. & intr. William Sweet (South Bend: St. Augustine's Press, 2001), 34-35.
11. Maritain, *La Loi Naturelle ou Loi non Écrite*, ed. Georges Brazzola (Fribourg: Éditions Universitaires, 1986), 201-203.
12. Maritain, "Natural Law and Moral Law," 70-71.
13. Ibid, 71.
14. According to John Courtney Murray, SJ, "The contents of his consciously protesting mind would be something like these. He is asserting that there is an idea of justice; that this idea is transcendent to the actually expressed will of the legislator; that it is rooted somehow in the nature of things; that he really knows this idea; that it is not made by his judgement but is the measure of his judgement; that this idea is of the kind that ought to be realized in law and action. Actually, this man, who may be no philosopher, is thinking in the categories of natural law. He has an objective idea of the 'just' in contrast to the 'legal.'" John Courtney-Murray, *We Hold These Truths. Catholic Reflections on the American Proposition* (New York, Sheed&Ward: 1960), 328.
15. Maritain, *Christianity and Democracy and The Rights of Man and Natural Law*, 115.
16. See paragraph J.B 2.2 for a more extensive explanation of natural rights and their relation to natural law.
17. An example would be "the good is to be done, the evil to be avoided." Another would be "one must render to each man his due." Maritain, *Man and the State*, 90; "Natural Law and Moral Law", 64; Aquinas, *ST* IIa IIae, q. 58, a. 1; *ST* Ia, q. 21, a. 1-3.
18. Their predicate is already implicit in the subject.
19. Maritain, *Man and the State*, 91.
20. Ibid, 93.
21. Ibid, 98.
22. *ST* Ia IIae, q. 94, a. 4, ad 1.
23. Maritain, *La Loi Naturelle ou Loi non Écrite*, 155-181.
24. As Jacques Maritain recalls, this problem is treated by Aquinas in question 67 of the Supplement to the III part of the *Summa Theologiae*. J. Maritain, *La Loi Naturelle ou Loi non Écrite*, 170-171,175.

25. Jacques Maritain, *Christianity and Democracy and The Rights of Man and Natural Law*, trans. Doris C. Anson (San Francisco: Ignatius Press, 2011), 106.
26. Ibid, 107.
27. Maritain, *Man and the State*, 94.
28. Maritain, *The Rights of Man and Natural Law*, (New York: Gordian Press, 1971), 71.
29. Ibid., 65.
30. Ibid., 81.
31. Ibid., 82
32. Abdulaziz Sachedina, *Islam and the Challenge of Human Rights* (Oxford: Oxford University Press, 2009), 41-80.
33. Anver M. Emon, *Islamic Natural Law Theories* (Oxford: Oxford University Press, 2010), 26-27.
34. Lawrence V. Berman, Review of *Averroes' Commentary on Plato's Republic* by E. I. J. Rosenthal, Oriens, vol. 21/22 (1968/1969), 439.
35. Sachedina, *Islam and the Challenge of Human Rights*, 61.
36. An-Na'im, *Toward an Islamic Reformation* (Syracuse: Syracuse University Press, 1990) 162.
37. Ibid, 97.
38. Paola Bernardini, *Abdullahi Ahmed An-Na'im's Human Rights Theory and Jacques Maritain's Natural Law Theory: A Comparative Study* (PhD diss., Pontifical University St. Thomas Aquinas, 2012), 149.
39. Ibid.
40. An-Na'im, *Toward an Islamic Reformation*, 163.
41. Ibid.
42. Ibid, 64.
43. An-Na'im, *African Constitutionalism and the Role of Islam* (Philadelphia: Pennsylvania University Press, 2006), 106.
44. An-Na'im, *Muslims and Global Justice* (Philadelphia: University of Pennsylvania Press, 2011), 103.
45. Ibid, 99.
46. Bernardini, *Abdullahi Ahmed An-Na'im's Human Rights Theory and Jacques Maritain's Natural Law Theory: A Comparative Study*, 150.
47. An-Na'im, *Toward an Islamic Reformation*, 164.
48. An-Na'im, *Islam and the Secular State* (Cambridge: Harvard University Press, 2008), 112-113.
49. An-Na'im, *Toward an Islamic Reformation*, 165-166.
50. An-Na'im, "Universality of Human Rights: Mediating Paradox to Enhance Practice," in *Human Rights Today*, eds. Miodrag Jovanovic and Ivana Kristic (Utretcht: Eleven International Publishing Co., 2010), 35.
51. An-Na'im, *Toward an Islamic Reformation*, 165-166.
52. Abdullahi Ahmed An-Na'im, "Civil Rights in the Islamic Constitutional Traditions: Shared Ideals and Divergent Regimes," *The John Marshall Law Review* 25:2 (1992), 268.
53. An-Na'im, "Universality of Human Rights: Mediating Paradox to Enhance Practice," 33.
54. Bernardini, *Abdullahi Ahmed An-Na'im's Human Rights Theory and Jacques Maritain's Natural Law Theory: A Comparative Study*, 158.
55. An-Na'im, *Toward an Islamic Reformation*, 163.

56. Ibid., 165.
57. A.A. An-Na'im, *Muslims and Global Justice*, op. cit. p. 77
58. An-Na'im, *Toward an Islamic Reformation*, 163.
59. Ibid., 162.
60. An-Na'im, *Muslims and Global Justice*, 99.
61. Maritain, *Man and the State*, 81.
62. Ibid, 245.
63. Maritain, "Natural Law and Moral Law," 66.
64. Ibid, 68.
65. Maritain, *Men and the State*, 111.
66. Bernardini, *Abdullahi Ahmed An-Na'im's Human Rights Theory and Jacques Maritain's Natural Law Theory: A Comparative Study*, 138.
67. Their view is endorsed by the 1981 Universal Islamic Declaration of Human Rights, whose Article 12 states: "No one, however, is entitled to disseminate falsehood or to circulate reports which may outrage public decency, or to indulge in slander, innuendo or to cast defamatory aspersions on other persons."

REVIEW OF *PLATO'S REVENGE: POLITICS IN THE AGE OF ECOLOGY* BY WILLIAM OPHULS (THE MIT PRESS, 2013)

Robert Chapman

Unlimited economic growth, resource scarcity, and natural limitations are familiar topics for William Ophuls. His earlier books *Ecology and the Politics of Scarcity* and *Requiem for Modern Politics* explored the contradictions between liberal political/economic philosophy and the natural world. He warned then that "man and nature are on a collision course." With the publication of *Plato's Revenge*, Ophuls returns to the above themes, only this time with a more nuanced *outline* of a solution he calls a "politics of consciousness" based on biological nature, physical nature, and human nature: "... I shall try to construct a new Aristotelian rule of life whose essential core is a politics of consciousness dedicated to the idea that ennobling human beings matters more than accumulating dead mater" (22). The central argument is that secular liberalism is incapable of guiding human action to avoid ecological scarcity and eventual collapse. Thomas Hobbes is reintroduced from his earlier works as the villain who successfully banished community and virtue from political philosophy: "... all modern polity is rooted in Hobbes's rejection of the classical conception of the polity – namely, that the state has a duty to make men and women virtuous in accordance with some communal ideal ... by making politics instrumental rather than normative, Hobbes and his followers set up a vicious circle leading to demoralization" (16). Ophul's heroes are "the ancient Gentes" who include Plato, Aristotle, Jefferson, Rousseau, and Thoreau – it is their common concern with the need for political virtue that unites them.

In Ophuls' reading of history, the Enlightenment *philosophes* never intended to liberate humankind from the natural order of things. Instead their intention, we are told, was freedom from religious tyranny: "... they were certain that human reason, once liberated from theology, would soon discover the moral order implicit within the cosmos" (6). History has proven them wrong! But we are now invited to right that wrong by finding the implicit moral order (natural law) in ecology, particle physics, and depth psychology. Ophuls' natural law, then, is a revision of that of the *philosophes,* who believed that scientific rationality would reveal a discernible moral order (21).

The ongoing revolution in thought that began in the late twentieth century, and provides the material for Ophuls' natural law, was driven by the "discovery" of the overwhelming complexity of biological, human and physical systems. The realization by ecologists, physicists, and psychologists that human culture is embedded in natural systems changed the focus from a mechanical interpretation of the cosmos to a more organic view, while at same time increasing the degree of complexity of those systems by orders of magnitude. It would not be an exaggeration to say we are in the midst of a Copernican revolution in reverse, minus the machine metaphor (not the author's language). Instead of removing the earth from the center of the solar system we are, in a way, returning it through a focus on natural processes and humans' indispensable relation to them.

As the subtitle of the text suggests, the master science for the twenty-first century is ecology. All living systems are subject to natural limitations; this is an indisputable ecological fact. It is also the cure for contemporary hubris (anthropocentrism), according to the author. What derailed the Enlightenment project was zealous attachment to a narrow, instrumental rationality. We became deluded into believing that nature could be conquered by technology to serve the purposes of human existence: "To understand ecology is to see that the goal of domination is impossible" (29). This is bad news for neoliberal economists whose goal is to grow the economy indefinitely through universal commodification. It is also a serious challenge to the liberal veneration of the individual, since ecology views the world thorough dynamic interdependent systems: "... there is no such thing as an individual life because organisms cannot by themselves sustain life" (34). The interconnection of these complex natural systems requires cooperation—"mutualistic symbioses" —not rights-based competition. Ecology articulates the organic metaphor through cooperation, natural limits, interrelationships, and the balance required by organic systems, and these natural properties all entail obligate ecological relationships—virtues like "humility, moderation, and connection."

If ecology dismisses the machine metaphor, physics, often considered the definitive model for science, belies it with even greater force. Ophuls approvingly quotes Sir James Jeans, renowned twentieth century physicist, to that effect: "Today there is a wide measure of agreement…that the stream of knowledge is heading towards a non-mechanical reality; the universe begins to look more like a great thought than like a great machine" (45). The twentieth century revolution in physics has provided us with a new vocabulary paradigmatically different from Newtonian mechanics and, to a degree, diverging from Einstein's macro model of cosmic order where God doesn't throw dice. Terms like chaos, uncertainty, nonlocality, indeterminacy, incompleteness, etc., take us far beyond the stable and predictable world we have become accustomed to. Yet beyond the universality of chaos, uncertainty, etc., scientists find order, self-organization and nonlinear processes remarkably similar to those found in evolutionary ecology. For example, Ophuls cites the findings of Noble Prize chemist Ilya Prigogine, who discovered that self-organization exists in inorganic systems (53). The theory of self-organization suggests "… a synthesis of physics, evolution, systems, and cognition that terminates in an explanation of how mind emerges from matter—or, more properly, coevolves with— matter" (55). If mind coevolved with matter and the natural laws directing matter are strongly implicated in mental processes, then there is little need for an ontology that separates the rational mind from the domain of human culture. Thus the virtues that apply to advance the ecological vision are the same for physics, namely "humility, moderation, and connection."

Ophuls concludes that the characteristics of the ecological vision are the same for physics: complexity, limitation, and interdependence. So it follows that the virtues derived from ecology apply with equal weight to physics: "... the new physics is fundamentally ecological ... all phenomena are part of a larger unified whole ... the wisdom and ethic of ecology emerge equally from physics" (60).

The chapter on depth psychology examines a dazzling array of studies conducted by psychologists and anthropologists, who conclude there are universal tendencies of the mind—archetypes. In the words of Carl Jung, a "2,000,000-year old man" lives in each of us (70). Ophuls focuses mainly on Jungian therapy, particularly the process known as individuation which, when successful, places limitations on the complex interaction between our instincts and emotions. Once this entanglement is harmonized, it is possible to construct a "politics of consciousness" based on a virtue ethic contained in the natural laws of ecology, physics, and psychology (93).

In order to reconnect the polity with nature, there must be a restoration of unity. Whereas depth psychology is about reconciling instinctual needs with the emotional contours of contemporary civilized life, we need further unification. Once again, Ophuls returns to classical Greek thought and reintroduces "paideia," and "politeia." The educational and political system he embraces is "... an Aristotelian rule of life that inclines our civilization toward a wise virtue instead of an unholy savagery" (98). Paideia is education of the whole person embedded in ecology and guided by the virtues of humility, moderation, and connection. There is no place here for neoliberal individuals who espouse unlimited economic growth and sanction a gross inequality among equals. Attempts to defy the natural laws of limitation and interdependence, for example, can only bring ruin to the commons.

It is a commonplace that the term "natural law" includes a variety of different ethical theories that break with the traditional Thomistic system. By favoring the "new" sciences of ecology, physics, and psychology over those that insist on an appeal to the will of a providential God, Ophuls breaks with tradition, but only by degree. What he finds in the natural laws of the new sciences is a way back to a more sane economic/political arrangement based on virtue. Behind the complexity of ecosystems lurks Plato's ideal state, where citizens find their niche and justice is the fulfillment of social roles; in the new quantum physics matter is not inert but alive, possessing thought-like processes, i.e. making choices between alternative possibilities of existence: "... the smallest units of matter are ... not physical objects in the usual sense of the word; they are forms, structures or – in Plato's sense – Ideas, which can be unambiguously spoken of only in the language of mathematics" (50); the same holds true for Jungian archetypes, the "... a *priori* structural forms of the stuff of consciousness ..." (85); so once again human flourishing can take place within the context of natural law determined by science, albeit a science that is willing to reconsider the long discredited idea of *telos*.

Even if Ophuls makes some immoderate claims about science, as I believe he does, his book is refreshing, well written (at times poetic), compelling and definitely worth reading if for no other reason than that he raises the familiar question with justifiable urgency: What does the term 'natural' mean in natural law theories?

REVIEW OF *ECONOMIC JUSTICE AND NATURAL LAW* BY GARY CHARTIER (CAMBRIDGE UNIVERSITY PRESS, 2009)

Richard Connerney

Never was our nation more in need of a book like Gary Chartier's *Economic Justice and Natural Law*. With the legislature deadlocked over moral issues such as workers' rights, taxation and health care, and the electorate blasted by a cyclone of competing economic philosophies and often unable to differentiate between media spin and common sense, the country would surely benefit from a set of overarching moral principles by which to evaluate the fiscal policies of our times. Chartier's book promises a pecuniary golden mean that avoids the ideological extremes of socialism and Randian objectivism, a conception of fiduciary morality that promotes worker's rights without the interference of a paternalistic state and prescribes fair distribution of income without fostering a culture of dependence.

Chartier's financial morality lies atop a short list of basic goods, incommensurable and non-fungible aspects of human fulfillment, which Chartier conceives in accordance with the new classical natural law theorists such as John Finnis, Germain Greisez and Robert George. Into this ground he drives the pylons of four principles: the Golden Rule, the Pauline Principle, Efficiency and Integrity, which guide his analysis of property, and Distribution and Work. An academic readership will find his treatment of at-will employment interesting, as at-will employment is the *de facto* condition of adjunct faculty at many colleges and universities. Chartier makes a convincing case that policies of arbitrary dismissal degrade the employee, harm the employer and cheapen the product, and he effectively counters objections based on an absolutist conception of property rights or a misunderstanding of the principle of Efficiency.

He is similarly thought-provoking when addressing discrimination, worker empowerment and corporate hierarchies. On the last subject, he offers a spirited, if ultimately quixotic, critique of top-down corporate power structures, which Chartier would replace with workplace democracies, arguing that an empowered workforce is more efficient and more capable of enhancing workers' well-being. Here, Chartier must overcome numerous objections from F. A. Hayek, Germain Grisez and Stephen Bainbridge, *et al.*, who offer various rationales for corporate hierarchy, e.g. requiring workers' participation in self-government is in itself an infringement on human autonomy (Bainbridge).

Unfortunately, Chartier falls into difficulty trying to explain why the egalitarian workplace democracies he imagines have not replaced corporate hierarchies over time through a Darwinian process of survival of the fittest. This reluctance to connect moral reasoning to the observable world constitutes the problem with Chartier's book. Although he has built a solid foundation for his arguments, the structure he places upon it lacks corporality. Chartier's rationalist approach is so bereft of real-life points of reference that his book on contemporary economic ethics never mentions the New York Stock Exchange, the Federal Reserve, Freddie Mac, TARP, the Euro or Bernie Madoff. This leads the reader to lament, echoing nineteenth century scholar and iconoclast Stephen McKenna's complaint about Plotinus's *Enneads* "Enchanted, you follow him through the lovely labyrinthine structure; you mount, breathless, by successive stairways of the spirit, each more pure, more tenuous, more aspiring than the last—but sooner or later comes a time when you ask yourself where the water closet is."

Nowhere are the limitations of this approach more apparent than in Chartier's treatment of health care. His argument rests primarily on the principle of Efficiency, largely ignoring the sticky moral issues associated with health care, e.g. rationing (the dreaded "death panels" of recent political discourse) and individual mandates that many see as an affront to personal autonomy. Chartier omits real-life accounts of indignities resulting from an unfair health care system—

patients denied coverage for the flimsiest of reasons, senior citizens abandoned on street corners when they are unable to pay their bills—and the lacuna leaves this politically pivotal issue floating in the ether as a bloodless abstraction.

Chartier concludes that health care should be a "communally funded" service with "private delivery." What this would mean in practice is unclear; the reader must assume Chartier intends a public health organization that outsources the administration of care to private firms. Addressing the myriad practical problems such a system would entail (and are now in evidence), he suggests only that communities refuse "… to provide sanction to occupational and institutional cartels that conspire to drive health care costs ever higher," and he thus reveals a Pollyannaish naiveté concerning both the nature of the private health-care industry and government's ability to curtail its worst behavior. At this point, the reader loses faith that Chartier's understanding of the issue is sufficiently grounded to inform the current debate in any meaningful way.

Economic Justice and Natural Law is plagued by stylistic problems. Chartier sometimes pushes his conclusions too far and makes statements—such as his advocacy of hand-outs to those "in search of bohemian freedom"—that put the entire book in danger of jumping the shark. Add to this an unfortunate habit of arguing obvious points, prose weighed down with needless jargon and a voice that seems, at times, to fall upon the reader *ex cathedra*, and this slim volume is a trial to get through.

It shouldn't be; the subject matter is timely, many of the arguments are convincing and the implications are potentially transformative. More attention to apt analogies and real-life examples would have made his book more readable without sacrificing depth or content, and Chartier would have produced a book both intellectually stimulating and affectively stirring. As it is, the reader must settle for one out of two.

CONTRIBUTORS

Paola Bernardini (University of Notre Dame) is Research Associate Professor and Associate Director for Research of Contending Modernities, a global research and education initiative examining the interaction among Catholic, Muslim, and other religious and secular forces in the world. She holds an Ed.M from the Harvard Graduate School of Education (Cambridge, U.S.A.) and a Ph.D in Philosophy from the Pontifical University St. Thomas Aquinas (Rome), where she was a Russell Berrie Fellow in Interreligious Studies.

Gregory Canning has published articles on Friedrich Nietzsche's philosophy of science and religion and is currently doing research on the philosophies of technology and science in twentieth century German thought. He is particularly interested in exploring the relation between freedom and technology in thinkers like Heidegger, Arendt, Jonas, and Spaemann. He plans to publish a translation with Alexander Schimpf of Spaemann's *Nach uns die Kernschmelze* (Klett-Cotta, 2011). He works as an adjunct professor at Assumption College in Worcester, MA, and is a Visiting Scholar at The Catholic University of America, where he received his doctorate.

Robert Chapman is Professor of Philosophy and Environmental Studies at Pace University where he is the Edward J. Mortola Scholar in Philosophy and Director of Environmental Studies. Chapman teaches courses in philosophy and environmental studies. He has presented papers on environmental philosophy at conferences in Albania, Canada, Cuba, Nicaragua and United States. Chapman has been teaching in the graduate program at the Steinhardt School of Education, New York University since 2008.

Richard Douglas Connerney is a freelance writer and teacher who lives and works in New York City. He is the author of *The Upside-down Tree: India's Changing Culture* (Algora, 2009). His work has appeared in *Salon, Tricycle: The Buddhist Review, India New England, The Newer York, Islam: Opposing Viewpoints, Gay and Lesbian Review Worldwide, Vera Lex* and other publications.

He was an overseas correspondent for the Institute of Current World Affairs in South Asia (2005-7), the senior editor of *Tricycle: The Buddhist Review* and a MacDowell Fellow (2007-8). He currently teaches philosophy at Pace University

Peter Furlong is a Visiting Assistant Professor of Philosophy at The University of North Carolina at Asheville. He works primarily in metaphysics, action theory, and the history of medieval philosophy. He has forthcoming articles in *International Philosophical Quarterly* and *Faith and Philosophy*.

James M. Jacobs is Professor of Philosophy and Assistant Academic Dean at Notre Dame Seminary in New Orleans, LA, where he has taught since 2003. He holds a B.A. from Harvard University and a Ph.D. from Fordham University. His major area of research is Thomistic natural law theory and more generally the need for a philosophical realism as a response to modern nominalism and skepticism. He has had essays published in such journals as the *American Catholic Philosophical Quarterly, International Philosophical Quarterly, Nova et Vetera,* and *Heythrop Journal*.

David J. Klassen holds degrees in law and philosophy including a Ph.D. in Philosophy from The Catholic University of America. He is a lecturer in philosophy at Corpus Christi College and Saint Mark's College in Vancouver, British Columbia, Canada. His research deals with questions of natural law and natural rights, the question of how objective values and ethical principles are known to us, and the place of religious belief in the public sphere.

Zachary Mabee is a graduate student in theology at the Pontifical Gregorian University in Rome and a seminarian for the Catholic Diocese of Lansing, MI. He studied philosophy and linguistics at the University of Michigan-Ann Arbor and has completed a licentiate in philosophy at The Catholic University of America. He will be ordained to the priesthood in June 2015.

Jeffrey M. Walkey is a doctoral candidate in systematic theology at Marquette University, Milwaukee, WI. Broadly, his research has focused on the retrieval of Thomas Aquinas for contemporary theology, metaphysics, and ethics. He has written articles on Thomistic metaphysics and hermeneutics, as well as the phenomenology of the French Catholic philosopher Maurice Blondel. Currently, he is working on his dissertation, focusing on the notions of faith and unbelief, error and falsehood.